ELEPHANT
WALK

To: Barry Cruickshank

Best wishes for the

long haul

Mar 21, 2009

ELEPHANT
WALK

**Balancing Business Performance
and Brand Strategy for the Long Haul**

Tendril Press

DENVER, COLORADO

Elephant Walk:
Balancing Business Performance and Brand Strategy for the Long Haul

www.InnovationHabitude.com

Published by Tendril Press™
www.TendrilPress.com
PO Box 441110
Aurora, CO 80044
303.696.9227

First Publishing May 2009

ISBN 978-0-9802190-9-8 Paper

Printed in the United States of America
10 9 8 7 6 5 4 3 2 1

Art Direction, Book Design and Cover Design © 2008.
All Rights Reserved by

A J Images Business Design & Publishing Center
www.AJImagesInc.com — 303•696•9227
Info@AJImagesInc.com

When you have got an elephant by the hind leg,
and he is trying to run away, it's best to let him run.

—Abraham Lincoln

CONTENTS

PART III
DEVELOP AND EXECUTE THE PLAN

Thanks to Jo for the elephants,
and to my friends at CEO Space
for their encouragement and support.

INTRODUCTION

It was a searing hot, dry, dusty day. The waist-high veldt grass formed an undulating yellow sea as hot breezes drifted by. Thick clumps of acacia trees appeared as islands emerging from the heat mirages and promised the only opportunity for shade. Our five-man unit came to a small depression surrounded by a dense wall of low shrubbery and acacia trees. Hours of trudging through thick grass and unfamiliar territory in the searing dry heat can make a weary man see things move that really aren't moving. Pale faces and lack of focus revealed early warning signs that we were dehydrated and possibly on the verge of heat stroke. Rest, water, and shade were urgently needed. We rounded the first clump of trees and stepped into the clearing. Looking about 25 yards ahead, our disoriented vision led us to conclude that what appeared to be a huge gray tree on the far side of the clearing had just moved. Venturing further into the opening, we gasped in unison as we realized the gray tree was actually a huge bull elephant standing in our path and looking directly at us.

The lone rogue male raised his trunk to sample the air for a better whiff of the strange scent that approached. Its huge ears were flapping slowly. With its raised trunk and eight foot long curved tusks, the bull elephant looked as large as a two storey house. Air rumbled through its chest. Aside from my own heartbeat, I could only hear the low, rumbling, vibration of heavy breathing which seemed to travel through the earth. I felt it through my boots. This massive animal could charge and cover the short distance between us in an instant if agitated for any reason. The heat from the overhead sun baked the red earth of the clearing. The chirp of cicadas in nearby trees sounded a shrill alarm to the danger we were facing. All eyes focused on the huge gray mass in front of us. Nobody dared make the slightest movement lest the bull noticed and didn't like it.

Out of habit, our team leader slowly raised his hand in a clenched fist to signal a stop, a useless direction which no one seemed to notice. We were frozen in our tracks. Yet the vibration was causing my boots to shake, or was that fear? At that moment any other order, like "Charge!!", or "Run!!" would have produced no result—no one would have budged, not even an inch. The assault rifles that normally made us feel invincible now seemed like pea shooters. If the bull decided to charge, drawing our guns would probably only make him angrier and we would never stop his charge at this short range.

None of the five-man team thought to raise a rifle. There we stood, five soldiers dressed in full combat camouflage gear, frozen in fear. Opposite us was the largest pile of flesh and bones and tusks any of us had ever seen. The bull pondered whether we were a problem. I prayed we would not be trampled into fare for hungry vultures and hyenas. The standoff continued for 15 long minutes. Then very slowly, the elephant turned its head and ambled off through the trees without another glance in our direction. The huge bull had determined we were not a threat and returned to its normal foraging and roaming activities.

A full-grown African elephant can weigh up to seven or eight thousand pounds with legs taller than a six foot man. On soft, moist earth, its feet leave huge pizza plate sized impressions. A casual stroll for an elephant occurs at four miles an hour, a fast walk for most humans. It can easily average 30 miles a day as it forages for food, which it needs in great volume to sustain its mass. At a run, the elephant can cover the ground at nearly

30 miles an hour for short stretches at a time. They have been known to travel as far as 70 to 80 miles in a day.

Logistically, this presents certain challenges. For such a large creature to cover such vast distances safely, it must sustain itself with plenty of food and water. During the dry season, elephants go from watering hole to watering hole, crossing dozens of miles of bone dry countryside, stopping briefly along the way to forage on scant patches of green leafy vegetation. How do they know where to go? How do they cover such large distances? Why don't they overheat in the African sun? How do they find each other?

Elephants maintain a balance and a gait that belies their impressive size and weight, and they step forward and shift their weight with amazing grace and fluidity. As long as the elephant is able to maintain its balance, keeping its feet working in a coordinated sequence, there is no stopping it from going where it wants to go. With an understanding of their power and how to use it, these huge creatures will often push over trees to reach the soft green leaves at the top that would otherwise have been out of reach. They will even cross deep water by walking along the bottom of a riverbed. When an area on the Zambezi River in Zimbabwe was flooded to create the Kariba Dam, elephants were seen using their trunks as snorkels, as they walked underwater for miles. The old river bed had been a traditional route they followed in the course of their travels. Even the flooded banks couldn't dissuade them from their chosen course. Covering vast amounts of territory unchallenged, the elephant is the true and noble lord over large domains of the animal kingdom. The lion may be the king of the jungle, but even it won't attack a healthy elephant. To challenge such a large and formidable beast would be senseless.

The Elephant Walk is a steady, purposeful gait. Despite its size, the elephant walks with graceful determination. Undeterred by obstacles, the elephant is steadfast in reaching its destination. The elephant will not be intimidated or distracted. The elephant has a clear direction, and it will arrive on time.

Your Business Is Like an Elephant

Think about this power and endurance in the context of your business. Consider the sum of all of the resources available to move your business in the direction and at the pace you desire. This includes people, customers, financing and systems—a formidable force if all the elements are aligned to perform in unison to achieve a common purpose. If you can achieve and sustain this alignment and focus on your mission, your competition will find it difficult to cause your business to veer off its intended path.

When the people and the parts are all working together, your business can develop tremendous endurance, even on scarce resources, and you will do it at a greater pace than you might ever have believed possible. Your people won't tire or be burned out by wasting effort on rework or direction changes that leave them feeling their goals are unattainable. When your business does the Elephant Walk, your reputation as a business will be akin to the elephant—lord over the business kingdom that you serve.

As consumers, we are aware of the power of a strong brand and the ability of such a brand to contribute to the strength and growth of the business. Our loyalty to specific brands directly affects our buying decisions. Think of your own choices when buying items like toothpaste, soda, denim jeans, and even automobiles. We defend our choices and promote them to friends, family, and neighbors. Brand loyalty for consumer products is driven by experience with the product: the product's performance and the image attained from using the product. This image is influenced heavily by advertising and promotions. Often, when consumer brand companies stumble, they make product or advertising blunders and loyal fans get turned off. This can be temporary, if the company acts to correct the mistake quickly.

Business-to-Business Companies and Brand Loyalty

Business-to-business service companies can also experience the benefits of a strong brand identity in customer loyalty, buying preferences, and referrals to other customers. However, the relationship with the customer is far more complex than consumer product relationships. Business-to-business brand loyalty is driven by experience both with the company and its people. This includes: product and/or service performance, sales, customer service, billing, account management and knowledge sharing. The challenge for business-to-business companies is having many customer touch points and often no tangible, visually identifiable product. Often, the service becomes integral to the daily routine of the customer and there is very little interaction with the service provider until something goes wrong and, inevitably, it does. Thus the only thing the customer remembers about the provider over time is the problems that occurred and efforts to get them resolved.

Performance metrics that measure internal systems may indicate a stellar level of performance and responsiveness, yet the customer may have a completely different perception. Business-to-business service companies must go above and beyond just satisfying the client's business transaction needs to create enduring positive brand loyalty. Business-to-business brand loyalty has less to do with spending money to build awareness than being committed to a complete, systematic and relentless dedication to an idea that touches a customer consistently across all communication channels and is sustained over a long period of time. Most often, when business-to-business companies stumble, they fail to align their entire customer-facing operational processes and people with their brand promise.

For customers of business-to-business companies, every form of communication they receive from their supplier, and every interaction with the company dictates their customer service experience. Unfortunately, this experience endures over time. Errors committed long in the past will remain part of the customer's experience with the business. Past negative perceptions persist regardless of how well the business is performing at present. Many companies mistakenly assume that as long as they have efficient customer service centers responding to customer calls and resolving issues quickly, customers will be happy with service overall.

Clearly for these companies there is a mismatch between customer perceptions and the business's understanding of their customers' needs.

The first important element differentiating your business is to deliver an experience consistent with your brand promise across every touch point customers have with your business. When those communication channels are aligned, delivering a consistent experience and message to your customers, you have achieved a high level of brand efficiency. When any channel fails to deliver on the brand promise, your brand efficiency decreases. When efficiency decreases, businesses will take a hit in lowered customer satisfaction and retention, willingness to buy, and overall financial performance. Vital energy in the form of human and financial capital is redirected to address the deficiencies. When brand efficiency is high, the company can focus its energy on serving the customer, innovating new solutions, beating the competition and increasing profits.

This book provides insights into the branding process, the value of executive leadership and the methods to develop and implement a winning brand strategy. Business leaders will get a framework to master the variables and systems of branding that play a significant role in building effective, sustainable and profitable growth. As a roadmap for executing and managing change, it provides examples and recommendations that businesses can use to achieve higher brand efficiency, profits and efficient growth. Focusing on the brand and building an efficient elephant-like business is essential for any business to reach its maximum potential.

PART I:

IDENTIFY THE PROBLEM/OPPORTUNITY

ELEPHANT WALK
PATRICK SMYTH

CHAPTER ONE

BRAND VALUE

Why should we pay so much attention to effective brand development? The purpose of branding is to create an indelible impression on the customer. Program positive attitudes so when the time comes to make a buying decision, customers already prefer your brand. Naturally, there are symbols that create a distinctive relationship with a brand. Take, for example, the Mercedes Benz three-pointed star. Most would instantly recognize it as a status symbol attached to automobiles of high quality, advanced engineering, and luxury—a reputation well-earned over many years of sustained performance by a company delivering top-quality automobiles to the market year after year. Now, take a look at the Nike® swoosh symbol: Immediately you are likely to recall their slogan "Just Do It," along with the attitude that it implies. If you are a basketball fan, you may recall Michael Jordan and the Air Jordan® shoes from Nike®, and an athlete who dominated his sport for quite a while—an outstanding example of the "Just Do It" attitude. Similarly, if you are a golf fan, you might imagine Tiger Woods wearing that swoosh—all the way to the bank.

Achieving this level of recognition is impressive; what value does it contribute to a business? Consider a 1995 study showing the average market value of public companies is 70 percent greater than their replacement cost.[1] This is often accounted for as *goodwill*: the equity earned by the company's brand recognition and reputation. According to an Interbrand report in *BusinessWeek* in 2006, 66 percent of Coca Cola Company's market capitalization is due to that company's brand. Best Global Brands reported that the Ford brand represents 87 percent of the market capitalization of the Ford Motor Company. Consider the case of Philip Morris:

> In 1989, Philip Morris paid $12.9 billion for Kraft, six times its net asset value. According to Philip Morris CEO Hamish Maxwell, his company needed a portfolio of brands that had strong brand loyalty [i.e., customer relationships] that could be leveraged to enable the tobacco company to diversify [i.e., financial relationships], especially in the retail food industry [i.e., trade relationships].[2]

Philip Morris paid billions for a set of relationships and expectations that would enable Philip Morris to conduct business in new ways in the future. A 1994 study by NYU concludes that the Kellogg's® brand name was approximately 68 percent ($15M) of the value of the company ($22M). And finally, a report by Stanford University Research indicates that Samsung earns over $127M a year from simple brand awareness. The brand awareness produces high profits—as the cost of sales for that $127M is extremely low.

"Brands are the global currency of business, in good economic times and bad," said Chuck Brymer, chief executive of Interbrand Group. In good economic times, there may be enough buyers to make many suppliers happy. When the economy turns and money is tight, strong brands continue to draw more business than weak ones. This holds true not only for customers who buy the company's products and services, but it applies to mergers and acquisitions as well. In financial terms, the value of a brand clearly can be a significant component of the value of the company. Brand value frequently increases the acquisition cost of a business. The price paid is substantially higher than the appraised value determined from the tangible assets of the company. The assumption is the brand equity, or goodwill, serves as a predictor of the company's ability to continue to conduct business in the future. The higher this value the lower the risk of failure, and the higher the value of the company.

However, to produce a meaningful and reliable assessment of the brand value of a business-to-business services company we need to assess the internal business processes. How effectively aligned are the various systems, functions and people? Are they delivering performance consistent with the brand promise of the company? The answers will develop a more clear understanding of the company's ability to perform in the future. Ignoring this assessment means ignoring real costs and inefficiencies that exist in the business resulting in unrealistic prices paid for brand value and underestimating the cost of expected productivity. Why pay a premium more tied to historical market awareness and market share, than to any real capability of the company to underpin its brand equity with real sustained performance? Since the brand contributes to the company's ability to generate and sustain future business, every element that falls short decreases business value. This includes inconsistencies internally or between the company and its customers' expectations for the future.

The good news is that factors influencing brand image in the market-place are largely within the control of the people who run the business. A 220-company study on Ad Value, by Leslie Butterfield, ed. (Butterworth Heinemann, Oxford, 2003) identified and quantified the key factors that influence corporate brand image.

TABLE 1.1 —

FACTORS INFLUENCING CORPORATE BRAND IMAGE

Advertising spending	30%
Size of company	23%
Low dividend	10%
Earnings volatility	7%
Stock price growth	8%
Other factors*	22%

*including other marketing components such as events and publicity, industry affiliation, product categories, message quality, etc.[3]

This illustrates that 52 percent of the factors influencing brand image are the result of processes and programs designed to define and articulate your brand message throughout your company. Activities involved with branding and communications and marketing and promotions support the brand overall. Investment in these areas can have a direct impact quickly. Other factors, although significant, take a long time to change or develop.

Through this brief analysis we conclude that a well-developed and executed comprehensive brand strategy will contribute directly to the value of the company and its stock price. The steps to accomplish this are adaptable to any business. The results will be measured in the improved overall performance in every function of the company, increased profits and continued growth in stock equity.

Examine the value of your business. How much of that value is attributable to brand value? What will your business be worth five or 10 years from now? What are you going to invest to develop your brand? What is the cost to your business of poor performance as measured by inconsistencies, errors, and failure to deliver on your brand promise?

CHAPTER TWO

BRAND EFFICIENCY

The concept of brand efficiency may seem vague and too complex to measure. Yet the issues are real and tangible and the impact can be illustrated clearly. A model of the impact of brand efficiency on sustained, profitable growth can be illustrated with the following. The terms are explained below:

Profit Potential = Net Profit X brand efficiency;

Where brand efficiency is the difference between brand affinity and brand entropy. This may also be expressed as:

Profit Potential = Net Profit X (brand affinity – brand entropy)

Each function, process, or transmission system in the company that executes the brand promise well (as experienced by customers) has a degree of brand affinity. Each one of those elements that is not delivering as expected, or where there may be inconsistencies between elements, contributes to brand entropy. Brand entropy is defined as the energy that is unavailable to do the real work of the company. This is vital energy that is being misspent to overcome errors or inconsistencies between the operations of the company and its brand promise. What is the cost of that energy in real terms?

Brand affinity is harder to quantify but the impact of brand power on profitability has been studied and reported by reputable firms such as Ernst and Young. In a study released in 2000, Ernst and Young estimated that brand power contributes approximately 5 percent to corporate profitability. A similar measure of the actual cost of the elements contributing to brand entropy can be calculated. When this brand entropy factor is subtracted from the brand affinity factor, the net result could be either a positive or negative number. If the result is below zero, then brand entropy, or the cost of poor performance, is clearly eroding your profits and your base business value. Your company is not living up to its full potential. We can then assume that any investment made to increase brand affinity, or improve performance, will accelerate profitability and growth. Whether or not we can establish effective models to measure brand efficiency this way, we can understand the impact that poor brand performance has on the bottom line.

For another analogy, look to the world of electronic communications, where entropy is defined as a measure of the random errors (or "noise") occurring in the transmission of signals. The efficiency of the transmission systems is measured as the effective throughput or capacity of any transmission medium minus the level of noise in the channel. In physics, entropy is a measure of the energy in a system or process that is unavailable to do work. To illustrate how brand entropy, or negative brand efficiency, can impact the overall efficiency and profitability of a business, it may be useful to look at a model of aerodynamics and the effect that resistance has on an object or a vehicle as it travels through the air.

As you see in figure 1.1 below, the larger the frontal area of the object the greater the resistance to the air flow and therefore the more resistance there will be. Higher resistance requires more energy to move through the air.

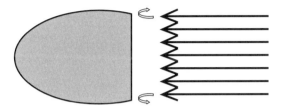

In figure 1.2, while the object may have a better design, a smaller frontal area and an overall sleeker shape, each raised flap adds to the resistance, creates turbulence, and increases resistance and energy consumption.

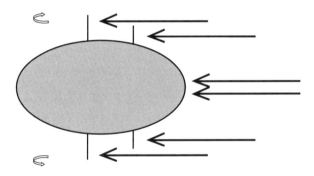

In figure 1.3, all the surfaces are cleanly aligned and the air flows easily over the entire object which now glides smoothly and effortlessly through the air, reducing the energy required to do so.

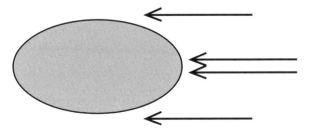

This concept of aerodynamics and drag can be applied to the level of alignment that businesses achieve with their brand promise. It demonstrates their brand efficiency, and the impact that poor alignment can have on increasing the energy, or consumption of resources, required to maintain business momentum. Poor alignment is a drain on resources and profit, while well aligned systems and processes reduce the drain on resources and can directly contribute to sustained, profitable growth.

The energy required for a business to move forward and accomplish its goals is directly related to the efficiency and consistency of the communications systems, and therefore the overall customer experience. In Fig 1.1, the company has a brand that is completely misaligned with its market. Even if this company provides a good product or service, the company will need to expend huge resources in sales and advertising and customer service to overcome resistance in the marketplace. In Fig 1.2, the company brand is well aligned, but certain functions or systems are not performing well, or they are not behaving in a manner consistent with the brand promise. This creates the 'flaps' which generate resistance. Each flap requires diverting resources to overcome the turbulence which drains resources away from selling and serving customers profitably. Finally in Fig 1.3, the company is well aligned across all communication channels and the resistance is low. Resources are freed to focus on serving customers and beating the competition. This scenario produces the highest return for every dollar spent.

We see that each business process, product or service, support system, employee, or communication not aligned with the brand promise, creates errors in the transmission systems of that business. Many businesses develop processes for measuring the internal efficiency of individual functions, processes or support systems. How often is the efficiency of these systems as a whole measured? How well do they perform in delivering the experience to the customer that matches the brand promise? If the customer experiences many facets of your business, from sales to the product, to service to billing, then how are all of those functions and processes aligned to produce a seamless customer experience? Each inconsistency or error against that objective requires energy in the form of human and financial capital that is unavailable to do the real work of the business. The cost of this entropy cannot be found in your monthly income statements or in the operational performance reports for any specific business function. As the organization evolves, these costs are simply assumed to be part of what it takes to make this business work. A wider view is needed to understand the impact.

The cost of poorly executing on a brand promise is real and can be measured. The elements of cost are often already measured by companies. They include rework, error correction, concessions, lost opportunities, and customer attrition. Each element contributes to increased costs in service, selling, support, and overhead as remedies are sought. These costs are multiplied when multiple elements fail. Each element or system that fails or is inconsistent or goes against the brand promise compounds noise in the communication and the impact of that noise on the customer. Each new error reinforces the negative perception from the first mistake, and the negativity snowballs.

If we assume there are errors in sales + service + promotions + website, we could assume a brand entropy factor of minus 4 (assume one point for each item). However, the compounding impact means that the effect of these errors is multiplied in customer perception, producing something like $(1+1+1+1)^2$ (i.e., the power of 2), or a brand entropy factor of 16, and not 4. Why is there such a compounding effect? Remember that for business-to-business customers, the sum of their experiences and communications with your entire firm over time serve to create their perception of your brand. When one element disappoints the customer, it is automatically compounded by another element-even though they may seem unconnected from your view inside your company. Left unchecked, the customer's disappointment grows and negative perceptions expand beyond the issues at hand to become a general perception of your entire business.

The cost of overcoming brand entropy, plus customer attrition due to poor performance, plus lost opportunity cost, all combine to create a drag on profitable growth. While the cost of brand entropy, or negative brand efficiency, may be difficult to measure, the impact of poor performance and quality on each of the transmission systems can be measured and many businesses have sophisticated processes, software and even Six Sigma quality improvement programs designed to measure and improve performance and increase profitability. Rarely, however, do these initiatives measure the effectiveness and consistency of communication and performance of systems in relation to the intended brand strategy of the business. Managing each of those issues in an isolated, and not in a holistic manner defined by the brand strategy, can result in a drain on energy and resources required to deliver sustained profitable growth.

One cost not easily defined, yet as real as those already discussed, is the cost of correcting a tarnished reputation or poorly aligned brand image. Customers will only believe your brand promise is real after a long experience of consistent performance. If this experience has been negative and you are now working hard to earn back the respect and trust of your customers, you have to recognize this fact and set long-term goals for measuring the effectiveness of strategies to change customer perception. Just like compound interest on a loan, you have to pay back the interest before you make a dent on the principle to build any equity. All that negative experience is the interest you have to "pay" so you can regain the privilege of brand equity and loyalty with your customers. Meanwhile, make sure that all new customers are experiencing your company the way your brand promise intends so that you don't build up more "interest payments."

CHAPTER THREE

ILLUSTRATING BRAND ENTROPY

The key to marketing and brand promotion is communication. If the brand is not aligned with customer expectations, then communicating brand values includes a large measure of noise in the transmission systems used to reach customers. What are those transmission systems? Every way your company interacts with customers is part of the transmission system. This includes the products and services and how those perform. Also included are: customer service, business systems, direct sales, billing systems, advertising and promotions, product literature, trade show demonstrations, web sites and executive leadership. Any malfunction can disappoint the customer and raise resistance to an otherwise well-executed brand. A poorly defined brand will lead to inconsistency in communication and performance throughout all of these systems, low business performance and a variety of inconsistent experiences for the customer.

Businesses can reasonably expect that their marketing department will communicate their brand through advertising, literature, and promotional activities. While this communication is important, it is just a small element of the totality of interaction that defines the overall customer experience. In addition, if marketing communication is assumed to be the only effort to define and promote a brand identity and build brand loyalty, then it would be out of sync with all the other systems in the company. If we don't recognize the need for alignment, we are building in, by design (or neglect) new sources of communication inconsistencies ("noise"), adding new costs to overcome them, and reducing the return on the investment. Clearly the brand promise should be defined and measured across all communications systems of the company. This strategy should include internal reward and recognition systems to encourage employee behavior consistent with brand values.

Let's examine some of the ways that broken communication channels can create noise that interferes with the desired experience for the customer, and the cost of overcoming them. How many times in business-to-business companies do we hear that the customer was sold something that differs from the company's ability to deliver? The list of potential gaps is very broad, including items such as product/service features, business terms, implementation schedules, service levels, pricing, and more. Apparently many sales people are prone to promising things that may be what they think the customer wants, but are beyond the scope of what the business can deliver. In business-to-business customer relationships, the goal is to develop a long term relationship with the customer. Generally, the longer it lasts, the more profitable the relationship. At the start of the relationship, what if the product or service does not meet customer expectations? What if the business terms or billing processes are cumbersome and prove difficult to navigate? What if the service levels are below stated standards? What if the product was not implemented on time as originally promised?

Each missed expectation requires energy and investment to overcome in order to guide the customer to an acceptable long-term path. This includes resetting expectations. The customer may experience significant shortfalls in the brand promise before the relationship really gets under way. The cost of building brand loyalty with that customer is very high and will continue to be a drain over a long period of time. The company may go to extraordinary measures to restore its reputation with that customer in an attempt to get the customer's experience closer to the brand promise. Remember, customers will include past experiences in their perception of the business, so these initial errors are costly and enduring.

Consider a company that provides information processing services to mid-market businesses in order to automate and improve the efficiency of finance and accounting systems. We'll call this fictitious company "Acme Financial Services". Acme prides itself on being the most reliable and accurate service provider in its category. Certainly these are desirable attributes of a financial services provider. Acme plastered messages about reliability and accuracy all over their marketing materials, and in their customer service centers. This theme of reliability and accuracy was central to Acme's brand promise. Acme's clients pay a monthly service fee to use this service, and there is only a small installation fee, due at the time the service is implemented. When the Acme Company considers the sales acquisition cost and startup costs for on-boarding a new client, they are able to recognize that profitability with each new client is reached after six to eight months of service, and sometimes a little longer.

Let's assume sales people are misrepresenting the Acme Company's capabilities. One of Acme's sales representatives has promised a customer certain functions that seemed reasonable, but were not included in the current product offering. Further, let's assume the sales representative told the customer that the service would be implemented and up and running in forty five days, consistent with general delivery schedules experienced with other customers. This, too, could be a perfectly reasonable assumption, but again it just so happens that when this customer order was signed there was an unusually high volume of orders and the backlog on implementation schedules increased accordingly. The contract was signed, and the project began, or so the customer thought. The first communication the customer received from Acme after signing the contract was a project schedule which indicated that the service would be implemented in 80 days. This is the first missed expectation for this customer. It also means that Acme's promise about reliability has been broken, and it comes in the form of a surprise—and not a happy one. Now the sales representative, the service manager, and, depending on the importance of this customer, perhaps even corporate management, need to spend time and money to prevent this business customer from changing its mind about proceeding. No matter what the resolution, the customer's perception about the reliability of Acme is tarnished.

Assume Acme managed to convince the customer to proceed and 80 days later, the new service was installed. Acme assigned their top implementation team to assure that this relationship remained on a positive track, and it all seemed to be working perfectly. Unfortunately, the customer discovered quickly that some of the features that they were sold did not, in fact, exist in this product. The customer called the customer service hotline for help on using and/or enabling the features in question. The service representative had no idea what the customer was talking about. Another major expectation missed, and this shortfall required a lot of attention from Acme management. Once again, Acme's reputation for reliability was damaged, but now they can add in damage to their other brand promise: accuracy. For a second time, the sales representative was called in, plus service management, and the corporate product manager so that the gap in understanding could be clarified and the customer's needs clearly defined. Considering the scope of the missing features and the cost to implement them, this customer was on the verge of switching to another supplier. If it were not for the huge investment in implementation and the time delay in getting another system installed and running, they would have bolted. This simple example is, unfortunately, a common occurrence with business to business service and software companies.

The costs to Acme of this one customer's experience are enormous. Acme's brand reputation cannot be repaired by any amount of discounting, concessions or advertising. Even if the customer remained with Acme's service for many years, there would be an underlying distrust, and they would be unlikely to ever recommend Acme's service to others. Customer loyalty and referrals is extremely valuable and can be expensive to recapture—in both money and time. In addition, Acme incurred large costs in time and effort, and lost opportunities dealing with these two simple errors. Resistance, or brand entropy, was created reducing brand efficiency which blocked Acme from investing that time and money more productively.

OK, now let's take the poor sales representative off the hook. Imagine, on the other hand, if Acme had installed this service on time and all the features met exactly the requirements that the customer expected. When the service was up and running, the customer was happy and believed they had made a wise choice in going with a company with the solid reputation for reliability and accuracy. They agreed to be featured in a press release and a case study, both of which were widely distributed. One month later, the customer called the customer service hotline for what seemed like a simple request to understand how to configure the reporting tools. The service representative answered the phone quickly and in a friendly manner, and even acknowledged the customer by name and thanked them for their recent purchase.

Unfortunately, this service representative was not knowledgeable in the area of the reporting tool. The call was referred to another representative who was not normally assigned to this customer. This representative was experiencing a busy day serving his assigned customers, and decided to direct the call to the next tier (Tier 2) of service. By this time, the customer had been on the phone for 15 minutes. The Tier 2 service team was very busy and they were not measured on the same rapid response metrics as the hotline service representatives. The Tier 2 representative recorded the customer's information and promised to follow up within the hour. Finally, the Tier 2 representative reconnected with the customer and attempted to convince the customer to use the reporting tool in a manner that did not match their needs.

The suggestion was not much use to the customer. Two and a half hours had passed since the original call. The customer was getting frustrated with the idea that either the product didn't do what was needed, or the service representative simply refused to make it so. Either way, the Acme Company's reliable and accurate brand promise was taking a beating. Once again, the sales representative and service manager intervened to resolve the issue and get the customer back on track. This service issue caused costly resistance and decreased brand efficiency for an otherwise well-executed business relationship.

Let's try another example. Assume that Acme had earned their brand promise of reliability and accuracy and was generally executing flawlessly. The marketing department delivered a direct mail campaign to promote some new optional enhancements that would bring in helpful revenue in the second half of the fiscal year. Existing customers were targeted with the mailed items and offered an incentive and a free cost-analysis modeling tool on a CD to help demonstrate the benefits of the new features. The response rate was high and hundreds of customers responded to the promotion and requested the cost analysis tool.

Acme sales and marketing departments were very pleased with this response and confidently raised their sales forecast for the second half of the year. A week later, calls poured in to the customer service hotline. The cost analysis tool had some serious errors which rendered it useless. The hotline service representatives had no knowledge of this tool, nor any ability to diagnose and fix the problem. Quickly the volume of these calls reached a point where the service manager brought the issue to corporate management's attention. Immediately, a letter of apology was written and sent to all customers who received the tool along with a promise to deliver a working tool within ten days. Meanwhile, Acme's reputation of reliability and accuracy was taking another beating. Acme had to spend a lot of money to correct this mistake while losing valuable time and trust with its core customer base.

Ten days later, the new tool was delivered as promised. Half of the customers had already decided they no longer trusted the new tool or the offer. They chose to wait until other customers installed the new features and Acme could definitively show the benefit. The other half resumed their analysis and, after considerable delay, finally purchased the new options. The immediate consequence of this error: the anticipated increase in sales shrunk to one-third of its original size. Acme would be experiencing a difficult fourth quarter and would need to make some spending cuts to meet their profit goals. One small flap created massive resistance and decreased brand efficiency which impeded the business' ability to compete and serve its customers.

These simple examples illustrate how failures, even small ones, can be costly and take a long time to overcome.

There are many subtle opportunities for the brand promise to be broken without any specific system breakdown or service failure. While all units can appear to be functioning properly and meeting performance standards, subtle factors can contribute to the customer experience not matching up with the brand promise. The impact will be just as damaging and costly to brand loyalty, brand efficiency, and require the long-term repair to rebuild the customer relationship. The consequence: It drains resources away from productive work and the bottom line.

The Relationship between Employee Culture and Profitability

Employee culture is a significant factor that will always impact your bottom line. The Service-Profit Chain, developed in 1997 by Heskett, Sasser and Schlesinger of Harvard Business School, establishes the interdependent relationships between profitability, customer loyalty, and employee satisfaction, loyalty, and productivity. The Service-Profit Chain is made up several key links: profit and growth are stimulated primarily by customer loyalty; customer loyalty is a direct result of customer satisfaction; customer satisfaction is dependent upon employee performance.

Satisfaction is influenced by the value of service provided to customers. Satisfied, loyal, and productive employees create value. Employee satisfaction, in turn, results primarily from high-quality support services and policies that motivate employees to deliver results to customers. Let's say you have high quality support services and polices, and your employee satisfaction surveys indicate your employees are happy. Does that mean your customers are in fact experiencing results that match or exceed your brand promise? Do satisfactory results really help you accomplish your goals of being the leader in your industry? What if the predominant culture of your employee base demonstrates a set of values that are not consistent with the values of your brand promise? What if different parts of your employee population that come into contact with customers have quite different cultures and values? Does your sales force demonstrate the behaviors, manner and style of your customer service organization? Inconsistent behaviors between employee groups, and between employees and the brand promise, create disjointed experiences for customers who will find that they must constantly adjust to your company's different styles, behaviors, standards of performance, and promises.

The customer will quickly conclude they don't know what you stand for, and they won't know how to describe their experience with you—perhaps other than "awkward". This makes it difficult to develop a sense of affinity and loyalty towards your company. The Service-Profit Chain model provides a foundation to assure that your employees are delivering results to customers. However, a focus primarily on employee support services and policies will not necessarily result in employees delighting the customer and delivering on your brand promise. Your company needs a defined employee culture and reward and recognition system that aligns behavior consistent with the brand promise of your business. This strong link and consistent behavior will strengthen the bond of loyalty with your customers, lower the cost of support service, and accelerate brand efficiency and sustained profitability. Employees need to relate their work with a higher purpose in order to align their decisions and actions with your strategic intent. Your company's vision and mission, as expressed through your brand promise, are the essential ingredients to accomplish employee motivation and empowerment.

CHAPTER FOUR

CUSTOMER PERCEPTIONS

In Africa, darkness comes swiftly at sunset—in the brief window of waning twilight, our patrol team found a small open patch and quickly laid down our sleeping bags on the soft, grassy earth and quietly prepared for the night's rest. The usual guard duty roster was established; each man staying alert for his two hour shift and then awaking the next and so on until dawn. The first sentry went to his post against a tree on the perimeter of the clearing. The rest of us were happy to be snug inside our sleeping bags under the soft light of the stars for a much-needed rest.

The first light of dawn came. The air was still cool and the sun had not yet risen. The only break in the calm silence of the early dawn was the distant whinnying of a herd of zebra.

The first man to be awakened by the change of light as the new day dawned sat up in his sleeping bag. He stretched his arms and yawned, getting ready to wipe away the cobwebs to be alert for the new day's activities. His eyes shifted from sleeping bag to sleeping bag to determine the state of his team mates. Then his gaze was arrested by a large dark green mound right next to one of the sleeping soldiers. He crouched over and began to crawl across the 15-foot gap to get a closer look at this unexpected mass.

"Holy crap," he uttered these words softly, yet it was still alarming enough to waken me and every other member of the group—not the words soldiers on a patrol like to hear out in the bush.

He couldn't help but notice something equally puzzling right next to his sleeping bag—a depression in a soft muddy patch of dirt two inches deep and large enough to fit a medium pizza. Startled by the realization of what this meant, he exclaimed, "Elephants!"

The sleepy group sprang into action. We shook the dew from our sleeping bags, and hustled with rifles in hand to react. Once aroused, we all saw what had raised the alarm.

Yes, the dark green mound was a small wheelbarrow sized portion of elephant dung! In the darkness, the team had unknowingly set their sleeping bags down right on the path used by the herd, and presumably many other animals, to get to their favorite watering hole two hundred yards away. In the blackness of the pre-dawn hours, a small herd of these large seven ton pachyderms nimbly tip-toed between five sleeping soldiers without touching, disturbing, or waking a single one. The team wasn't sure whether they should be thankful that nobody had been squashed, or more thankful that the elephants' calling card hadn't landed on some poor sleeping soldier's head.

Committing what would normally have been an extremely serious offense, one sentry had fallen asleep during the night and the sentry schedule had been broken. Thus the events of the night went by completely unnoticed by these five tired soldiers, who remained soundly asleep until roused by a whispered alarm. The hapless guard who had fallen asleep was thoroughly chastised by all for failing his duty to his post and to the team. Secretly, his consolation came from the awareness that he could well have been a lone guard on duty faced with a herd of elephants marching right through the camp. What was the appropriate response to that?

These elephants had taught us an unexpected and powerful lesson. We already had a lot of respect for their awesome size and power, but now we learned of the amazing gentleness, grace and agility these animals demonstrated passing through the camp in the night. When they realized our troop was no threat, they simply walked quietly on through to their destination—the watering hole. Amazingly, they did this without touching or waking any of the team members. This was a defining moment that permanently altered our perception of elephants.

Customer perception about your business is something that you must define, influence and manage. Even if you think you have your value propositions, market positioning and your brand promise well defined and communicated to your employees, you may still find that customers are not as satisfied as you believe. It is quite possible that your values and brand promise make sense to you and your management team, and, perhaps, to certain members of your target customer population. What if the customer's definition of these ideals does not match the standards and measures outlined by your company?

Imagine that the Acme Company had successfully convinced senior decision makers to buy a service based on a promise of reliability, accuracy and a set of values that were designed to match that promise. All the benchmarks and standards of performance were perfectly aligned with the executive customers' needs. After the service is installed and operating, the day to day interactions and operations are managed by financial support administrators, financial analysts, and billing/operations personnel.

How do the customers measure reliability and accuracy and all the values that Acme has espoused? Perhaps to customers, reliability means reaching a knowledgeable person on the first call every time, not some measure of system availability and access. Perhaps they place a high value on receiving technical news updates to help them stay abreast of developments and trends in their business including changes that affect their jobs. What would be the impact on brand loyalty and perceptions about reliability if Acme were to provide such a valuable information service? The cost of not recognizing these small nuances is much more difficult to quantify because this issue really refers to the concept of opportunity cost. That is: what is the benefit we could have recognized and provided had we better aligned our brand promise with the customer? How much are we spending to overcome perceptions of inconsistency and the resulting weakened brand loyalty with each customer? We do know that these costs are real and they diminish brand efficiency and, therefore, profitability. Once again, the brand promise needs to be clearly articulated and consistent across all customer touch points and adapted to the roles and functions of both the customer and your employees. In a document describing their services, JP Power included this statement:

> Once the organization has reached a point where each customer experience is consistent across all organizational and functional channels, it is ready to make a leap to world-class customer experience at a strategic level.

Customer Touch Points

Consistency across all touch points requires:
1. A clear message articulating vision/strategy
2. Consistency across all customer touch points:
   sales, marketing, service, operations, web, billing, corporate, product, R&D, and all other functions
3. Consistency through each layer and role—executives, staff, production line
4. Accurate interpretations across all functions
5. Frequent, continuous direct communication from the top
6. Consistent culture and personality throughout company.

Essentially, this all boils down to consistency and integrity. Consistency: to ensure a consistent message across all of the touch points. Integrity: to ensure the company does for customers what it has promised to do. Many companies have systematic and rigorous metrics for measuring the performance of customer service centers. Large call center operations display the number of calls, average hold time, time to respond, and other metrics designed to encourage the entire service center staff to maintain the highest levels of operational efficiency. But do these metrics verify the customer is having the optimal experience? Have we clearly distinguished how effectively we are satisfying customer needs, or are we simply measuring how quickly we answer the phone and move on to the next call? Did we merely apply a "quick fix" that was not much more than a band aid on the issue, thereby guaranteeing that the customer will need to call again the next time the same problem arises? What if we spent a few more minutes helping the customer to resolve the issue or empower them by teaching them the ways to work around or fix the problem themselves, including walking them through your website's online knowledge base? What would happen to customer loyalty and perceptions about service and your product?

Knowledgeable customers tend to have far more favorable perceptions about the products they use because they know how to get more out of the product than a novice user, and they know how to work around simple issues that arise. They are empowered, and their confidence translates into positive perceptions about the company and its products. If the customer has to repeatedly call your support team about the same issues over a period of time, you will convince them that not only are you unreliable, but you are not particularly concerned about them—or you would have resolved the issue the first time. This erodes trust in the service, and the company's reputation, and weakens the brand.

A friend of mine related his own experience with customer service to help illustrate this issue. He had, over time, acquired two personal computers from a leading computer company that had a reputation for delivering high quality, low cost, and reliable service. He lost the power cord for his computer and called the company's technical support hotline for assistance. The first support person was in India and did not seem to understand my friend's request. The rep tried to transfer the call to someone else, and my friend was put on hold for 40 minutes. My friend hung up the phone and retried the support hotline number several times until a representative in America finally answered the phone. This person seemed to recognize the situation and the details of the request and sent out a new power cord immediately. A power cord arrived 48 hours later, as promised, but it was not the correct part for his computer. My friend said he would never buy a computer from that company again. Not only is his trust in that company and its reputation broken in his mind, he is obviously quite willing to share that story with others, thereby extending the damage and cost of this one error. Sometimes a small mistake can lead to a complete breakdown of trust, particularly when coupled with a frustrating service call experience.

As we saw earlier, business-to-business service companies often have two different customer relationships with each client. Senior executives are the decision makers. All of the early communication, sales and value propositions are directed at them. The service provider correctly believes that their sales and marketing messages must address issues that are important in the executive suite. The sales process and the service results often require knowledge of the client's business and expertise in the process. However, the end-users of the service are often clerical and operations support people, as well as middle management and the staff supporting them.

Service providers can fail to recognize the importance of building relationships with support staff. These workers can have an influence on future buying decisions at their company and, through associations with peers, at other companies as well. Providers often overlook them completely, or arrogantly assume they are not important and relegate the relationship building to low-level staff. There is often limited interaction with these workers and the provider's management team. The tendency to ignore these key players does not go unnoticed, and the support personnel will develop negative perceptions of the provider. When management is considering an upgrade, or adding new services and asking support staff for feedback, what will they say? When they show up at trade conferences and participate in discussion groups and network with peers, what are they likely to say about your company? Arrogance can have a seriously detrimental impact on brand loyalty. Correcting this impression can take more time and more money than any customer service error because it fundamentally defines your culture in the eyes of your customer.

Do your customers even know who you are, what you stand for, what you aspire to be, and what your vision of the future means to them? Maybe your business was started with a unique and highly-desired service, and you have experienced phenomenal growth over the last five years. Your success formula is working, and it seems to be unstoppable. Now that the market for your service is validated, the big companies with deep pockets have decided to move in with investments that make you shudder. It is possible that you never defined a brand promise because you never saw the need to do so. Your product or service sold itself, and now the competition is moving in and offering clear value to your customers and, by default, defining you in the process.

You now find yourself scrambling to respond by getting back in touch with the customers who are loyal to your product. Your product was the first of its kind and has acquired loyal users, but very few of these users have a clear understanding about your company or your ability to address their needs going forward. They simply don't know who you are. This situation is not too different from consumer brands. You may love your car, but you have no idea about what it may be like to work with anyone at the auto plant. Your experience with the car company is created by daily use of the car and by the dealer service relationship. You may make assumptions about the manufacturer from that experience, but you know nothing about the true nature and capability of that company.

Your business will need to spend time and money to develop a brand promise that connects the customer with your products and your vision of the future. If all this time you have only developed a de facto brand image, your brand needs to be clarified, defined and incorporated into your new strategy.

Perhaps your business has been providing transaction services to a loyal base of customers for 35 years. You have a significant share of the market, but you've noticed you're increasingly under price pressure and volume is starting to decline. Your success formula isn't working anymore and new players are emerging. Your market is being redefined. Your transaction service, valued by customers for many years, may have become a commodity and customers are looking for more value and integration with other applications, and/or information access for support to improve their business processes.

Your new competition understands this, and they are redefining the market around integrated solutions and decision support services. For them, transaction services are almost worth giving away as long as they are able to extract much higher value for their integrated solutions. In spite of your ability to deliver outstanding, reliable service, the value equation is changing. Loyal customers are beginning to migrate to the new providers who seem better able to address these new needs. Your brand promise and identity served you well for many years as customers placed a high value on your service, but it is now old, and no longer relevant to the needs in the marketplace. You need to invest both time and money to refresh your brand, reconnect with your loyal customers and communicate your ability to address their needs in the future.

Mergers and acquisitions are a common strategy in today's business climate. Perhaps your company is one of those who decided the way to grow rapidly and expand into new adjacent markets is to acquire companies with products and customers in each space. You acquired several small companies, with each acquisition deal including complex earn-out provisions with the principals, and growing internal resistance to assimilating with your company. You are now operating with multiple disparate identities, logos, cultures, customer service centers and even sales forces. Sometimes you even have different sales people calling on the same customer to sell different solutions as part of this new "integrated solutions" strategy you followed to justify your acquisition. Your brand promise is muddled at best. Your success formula requires that you integrate these companies to realize the long-term benefit of these acquisitions.

At this early stage, you are spending more money to acquire customers and overcome confusion than you might have spent just selling more of what you had before the acquisition. You have left it entirely up to the customer to try to understand your company and its capabilities. Your customer is hearing and experiencing widely different, possibly conflicting, messages and business processes in its dealings with your company. The result: frustration and confusion. You will spend a lot of time and money trying to rescue important relationships you had previously viewed as solid. Your competition is having a field day explaining just how messed up your company is and how much simpler it will be for your customers to replace you.

You will need to invest time and money to integrate these businesses as rapidly as possible. This includes integrating all the customer facing components, defining your new brand promise, and fully aligning every business unit and every employee in the company with this new brand promise. You have redefined your business by acquiring all of those companies. Now you need to clarify a new strategy and brand promise based on these new assets. This should be done even if some of the services cannot be integrated for some time. The customer should never be put in the position of trying to sort out the differences between your sales representatives, different technical implementation personnel, different billing systems, and different support service hotlines that you acquired supposedly for their benefit. No matter how strong your brand promise and customer loyalty may have been, the failure to integrate and align acquisitions will surely damage that loyalty rapidly.

In each of these scenarios, the result is that your brand is not well defined and not in alignment with your customers, or perhaps even with your own capability. In every case, there is a significant investment required to correct the situation and get your company performing according to its brand promise and its full potential. Could any of these extraordinary investments have been avoided? Certainly. Companies need to stay abreast of changes in the marketplace and recognize the need to develop a brand promise and maintain a systematic effort to ensure that every facet of their business delivers on this promise. This means certain costs should be incurred earlier, yielding large returns in customer loyalty and brand efficiency allowing the company to deftly fend off new competitors as market needs change.

The long-term benefit of maintaining a sustained, broad-based branding initiative is lower customer acquisition and support costs, which yields profit improvements and allows companies the flexibility to make changes as needed over time. The cost of sustaining a brand promise across every function of a business is simply a matter of aligning every function, its measurement and reward systems, and customer outcomes, with the brand promise. This cost is lower than the cost of having each of the functions and units operate with independent and disparate measurement and reward systems and customer outcomes. In the case of acquisition strategies, even strong brands can be completely destroyed when the acquiring companies fail to integrate the acquisitions into the business and the company brand promise. The cost of recovery for these companies is enormous and lengthy, and much of that cost is avoidable.

1. Tom Duncan, Driving Brand Value, pg. 4

2. Ibid

3. Ad Value, Leslie Butterfield, ed., Butterworth Heinemann, Oxford, 2003, "How advertising impacts on share price," James Gregory, pgs. 17-25.

4. Employee Commitment Remains Unchanged..... Watson Wyatt Worldwide (2002).

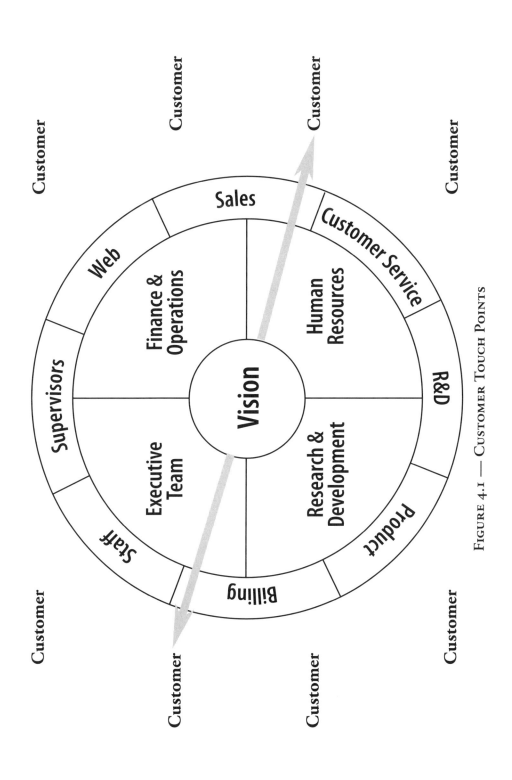

FIGURE 4.1 — CUSTOMER TOUCH POINTS

PART 2:

IMPORTANT ELEMENTS OF BRAND

CHAPTER FIVE

BRAND FOUNDATIONS

Many companies recognize the need to have a Mission Statement, or a set of values or principles which guide the behavior of employees. Unfortunately, very few seem to recognize that all of these are essential in building the brand promise and ensuring that it will become reality. Each element plays a unique role, and each needs to support the other in order to become relevant to all key stakeholders. The elements include: vision, mission, values statement, positioning statement, and value propositions.

Vision

A Vision Statement is one of the most important elements in defining your company's brand promise. Jack Welch, former head of GE, expressed the importance of having and executing a compelling vision. "Good business leaders create a vision, articulate the vision, passionately own the vision, and relentlessly drive it to completion." The Vision Statement is the very top-level message that clarifies your strategy and brand identity. Everything else that you communicate about your goals and objectives should be aligned to this vision. A Vision Statement is not a statement of objectives (the mission), nor does it include specific deliverables, time frames, or measurable results. While it is not a specific statement of objectives, a Vision Statement clarifies the purpose of the company and encourages all internal decisions and objectives to be consciously and purposefully aligned with it.

A good Vision Statement makes a promise about a future state that your business will achieve. Sometimes the Vision Statement is used to construct a tag line for advertising and promotions to help reinforce the message on an ongoing basis. The Vision Statement offers a compelling opportunity for the customer to participate in a future that will, by the leadership of your company, be substantially improved or advanced in a unique way.

Let's try an example to illustrate the power of vision. A welder at a shipyard is working on assembling several giant steel plates. A man walks by and asks the welder, "What are you doing?" The welder replies "I'm welding these steel plates." The man continues walking and finds another welder and asks him the same question. This second welder replies "I'm building the hull of a large ship." The man continues walking and finds a third welder and asks him the same question "What are you doing?" To this, the third welder replies, "I'm building the USS Ronald Reagan, the most advanced aircraft carrier in the world so that America's finest men and women can keep the rest of us safe at home." Clearly, the third welder understands the higher purpose for his work—that's vision. Which of these welders is most likely to perform the highest quality work?

When Bill Gates said his goal was "To put a computer on every desktop," or "Information at your fingertips," he made audacious statements with a never-ending game plan. He clarified the intent behind Microsoft's business strategy, and he enabled everyone inside the company to focus their energies on these common goals. It also clarified for customers what they can expect Microsoft to be in the future. This empowered them to decide how they want to participate with Microsoft in the vision and what form their relationship might take. Archer Daniels Midland (ADM) Corp.'s vision statement reads: "To Unlock the Potential of Nature to Improve the Quality of Life". Again, this statement makes a bold promise and it has a never-ending game plan. You can expect that regardless of the specific accomplishments made by ADM along the way, this statement will still be valid a year from now, five years from now, or even 20 years from now. It clearly focuses the company in a specific domain with a specific purpose. Yet, it does not attempt to quantify or put a time-limit on the desired outcomes. These are characteristics of powerful vision statements. The ADM statement has an additional positive quality in that it proposes an outcome, or a benefit, to the world at large: "… to Improve the Quality of Life." Who doesn't want an improved quality of life? ADM wants you to know that they can be relied upon to provide that benefit. This is the starting point of establishing brand affinity with customers. A good vision statement connects the customer's vision of their future with your promise for that future. If your customers believe that your purpose and promise are intimately connected to their future, you have the basis for developing a strong, long, loyal and profitable relationship.

Brand affinity is not the result of a handful of executives sitting around having a cocktail after work dreaming up all the cool names and terms that can be attached to your business or products. Nor is it the result of an expensive advertising agency's creative guru. It cannot be generated through any internal process that ultimately gets adopted through a battle of egos. Nor can it emerge through an unwillingness to depart from the sunk cost involved with creating these brand identity elements. It can only be ahieved by understanding the industry, marketplace and customers that you serve.

Relentlessly execute the brand vision with effectiveness, and it will have a turbo charging effect on your bottom line. As each element of your brand strategy achieves a measure of affinity with your customers, the effort needed to communicate, distinguish, and clarify your relationship and purpose with them is reduced. Each element of affinity supports the others and the benefits compound as communication of your brand promise becomes more efficient and more effective. Thus, the cost of communication is reduced as you create awareness and build brand equity. You will build longer-lasting relationships with your customers and lower the cost of acquiring and supporting new customers. This translates to increased profitability.

Now, if you can learn one more key step, you can add an indelible ingredient that has the potential to permanently connect you and your customers. Take a minute to internalize this statement: "If you want your customers to be raving fans of your business, you must first become raving fans of your customers." If you can create a unique style of customer relationships, adding a "coolness" factor to your brand, your customers won't just be loyal, they will become devoted fans. You will then have all the ingredients for sustained profitability through good times and bad.

Mission

A Mission Statement should be succinct and define the objective of the company. All too often, the mission is either too vague, or far too complex for anyone to readily comprehend and translate into action. Consider a Mission Statement like: "Our mission is to deliver the best service in the industry to our customers." Is this vague enough? Being the best at service is an aspiration, but it says nothing about what your company does. What is it that you are trying to accomplish as a business? How would these words clarify your purpose and allow customers to recognize that you are in fact doing that? Try this one: "Our mission is to be the leading provider of wholesale, low-cost, recycled, un-dyed paper product packaging material to the non-foods retail consumer goods industry in Northern California to demonstrate our commitment to environmental protection and eliminate the use of chemicals that add costs to the production process and produce harmful wastes, and to protect the earth's forests." While this is specific enough, it is also way too long-winded. It is way too limiting and confusing as it muddles the company's environmental concerns with its purpose. Consider some well-known company Mission Statements:

Southwest Airlines: "The mission of Southwest Airlines is dedication to the highest quality of Customer Service delivered with a sense of warmth, friendliness, individual pride, and Company Spirit."

Dell: "Dell's mission is to be the most successful computer company in the world at delivering the best customer experience in markets we serve."

eBay: "eBay's mission is to provide a global trading platform where practically anyone can trade practically anything."

Nokia: "Connecting people."

In each case, the purpose of the company is clear, even though some are more precise than others. The first three clearly characterize the company's type of business whereas Nokia leaves it up to the audience to associate their brand name in cellular telephony with their mission. Nokia's mission also does not restrict them to cellular technology, but their purpose of connecting people is very clear. Good Mission Statements should state simply what you do. Southwest Airlines' mission also articulates the style in which they will accomplish their mission, thereby setting the expectation of the experience that employees should deliver to customers. Adding that aspect of personality and personal relationships sets them apart from others who might claim quality of service.

Values Statement

Values Statements serve as guiding principles for the behavior and decision making that employees of the company will follow as they conduct business. These statements need to be similarly to the point and aligned with the mission of the company.

For example, Southwest Airlines includes their values in a statement to employees:

We are committed to provide our Employees a stable work environment with equal opportunity for learning and personal growth. Creativity and innovation are encouraged for improving the effectiveness of Southwest Airlines. Above all, Employees will be provided the same concern, respect, and caring attitude within the organization that they are expected to share externally with every Southwest Customer.

The connection with Southwest's mission is clear and even stated directly. Not only can customers count on being treated a certain way, but the company promises that employees will receive the same considerations they are expected to deliver to customers. The Service-Profit Chain is directly aligned in this statement and judging by Southwest's performance as the leading US airline in customer service for several years in a row, these values are indeed practiced well by the company.

Often, companies have written mission and values statements that a large number of the employees in the company have never seen. The HR director will tell you that some time ago they did produce those statements, and they posted them in buildings on signs and posters and may even have given new employees a brief pamphlet designed to inform them of the company's mission and values. In five years, even with a relatively stable 10 to 15% annual attrition rate, a large portion of your employee population will be new to the company. Further, in five years, most companies experience a lot of changes in organizational structure, leadership, and perhaps even market focus and product direction.

How has the company's mission and values statement evolved, and is it communicated regularly and consistently to every employee? Are employees empowered to adapt the key tenets of the Values Statement and apply it to their role in the company? Are the mission and values repeated and reinforced by executive management frequently in business updates, meetings, and other internal communications? Do company objectives, performance measures, and rewards and recognition line up with these values?

For any strategy—including mission and values—to succeed, it must be woven into the fabric of every aspect of the company. It must be communicated, understood, and implemented in every function, at every level—from the very top to the very bottom. Repetition is key: keep the message at the front of everyone's minds. Don't let it slip into the background. Also, there must be some flexibility and adaptability, so your strategy can evolve as market conditions change.

Aligning Behavior

Aligning behavior is probably the most important aspect to consider in understanding how to successfully implement and execute your brand promise. Top management must conform to that behavior and demonstrate it every day. Then it must be institutionalized through all of the performance measurements, management, and reward and recognition systems. Does the CEO weigh-in strategic questions and decisions against the vision and brand promise of the company? Does the CEO hold his direct reports accountable for performance and behavior that aligns with the brand promise? Does the CEO's own behavior model the behavior implied in the statements that have been issued to all employees in the company? If the answer to any of these questions is "NO," then how can anyone expect employees to follow the guidelines in the Mission Statement? Who will be their role model? What will happen to a company and its customers over time when the behavior of the top executives does not match their Mission and Values Statements?

As a dramatic example, let's consider the four key values communicated in Enron's mission statement: "Respect, Integrity, Communication and Excellence." This statement was intended to clarify the type of behavior that was expected at Enron. When these core values were violated at the top, what hope was there of the rest of the brand promise being delivered to customers? What was the cost of Enron's top management not following the values they espoused? Many lost their jobs and their reputations. Some went to prison.

Leading by example is perhaps the most powerful way for employees to fully grasp the meaning behind the words of the brand promise and the level of commitment within the company to assure the brand promise is delivered successfully. Employees will align their own behavior quickly, not out of fear, but because they want management to view them as "team players" and notice their skill as they execute the strategy as expected. Internal rewards and recognition systems should reinforce these desired behaviors.

Just remember to first ensure that the brand promise is aligned with your customers' values and you create expectations that you can and want to deliver. Some of the areas to identify include expectations about the purpose, quality, responsiveness, and customer care.

Integrity

The one underpinning principle of any other value—business or personal—that you may follow is integrity. It may be ironic that one of the few places that the word integrity appears in your company is at the water cooler. Yes, you intentionally hung a poster announcing the value of integrity at the location most famous for gossip. How's that working for you? Is it just a poster decorating the wall, or does integrity have an actual role in your business? Does your company operate with high moral character? Check out these six principles to find out.

When asked, most people will equate integrity with honesty. Honesty means ... well, we all know what honesty means: to be one with what is. But most of us struggle to define integrity. It's not just being truthful. Integrity comes from the Latin word *integer* meaning whole, or complete. But what does it *mean* to have integrity?

John Maxwell, author of several leadership books, offers this broad definition, "Integrity commits itself to character over personal gain, people over things, service over power, discipline over impulse, commitment over convenience, and the long view over the immediate."

Let's take a look at each one of the key phrases in Maxwell's statement:

Character over personal gain

Character builds the trust required to gain support from employees, suppliers and customers alike, and to build strong and sustainable organizations. If your climb to the top of the corporate ladder is built on personal gain alone, then you will have not developed any trust within the organization. Instead, you may have built a culture where everyone is looking only at what is in it for them. Who, then, is working in the best interest of the customer? Ask yourself if you're doing the right thing, not just what is right for you.

People over things

Businesses are run by people…by all the people in the company. Customers buy from people. People provide service and support to clients. Focus on the needs of your people to ensure you have a highly-motivated and empowered workforce. This must take a higher priority than fancy buildings, furniture, and the accumulation of objects. Your people will put your company first when you put them first.

Service over power

Leaders who operate only by exerting control over people communicate their selfish desires clearly and blaze a trail of resentment and distrust as they push their agendas forward. By contrast, leaders who focus on serving their employees and their organizations will build loyal and highly effective teams. Leaders must place a high priority on helping their people be more productive. This includes providing clear direction, allocating resources, assisting in problem solving, giving advice and counsel, and breaking down barriers. Building this level of trust will be vital when challenging the organization to new goals or to meet unexpected changes.

Discipline over impulse

Occasionally opportunities present themselves that would appear to offer an immediate gain. In order to benefit from an opportunity, a disciplined leader must determine whether it would require any compromise in values, risk any relationships, or break any trust before moving forward. That discipline keeps the leader and the organization on an even keel.

Commitment over convenience

Commitment requires a relentless pursuit of your mission every day and in every decision you make, even when it is inconvenient. To keep the organization on its course, leaders must demonstrate a persistent pattern of communicating, planning and executing their goals over time.

The long view over the immediate

Sometimes a "short-cut" might appear more convenient and provide more immediate gratification. If it takes the organization away from its vision, the long-term impact of that decision is very costly. Leading with integrity means that you evaluate every decision or course of action for consistency with the long-term vision and direction of the company.

The weekly financial magazine, *Barron's*, defines integrity as "The quality characterized by honesty, reliability, and fairness, developed in a relationship over time. Customers and clients have much more confidence when dealing with a business when they can rely on the representations made."

Focus on integrity first, and on its true meaning of wholeness and completeness, to build an organization where honesty and trust are steadfastly in place and supporting every aspect of your business. Better yet, you will create a sustainable, profitable enterprise that can withstand and endure the many challenges it will face.

To assure the success of your brand strategy plan:

1. Define your vision (identity) / mission (purpose) / values statements.
2. Communicate each to everyone, repeatedly.
3. Live/demonstrate it—employees mimic your actions first, not your words.
4. Execute consistently across every facet of your business.
5. Lead by example and make every employee accountable—it starts at the top.
6. Connect your values to your customers to assure that their experience matches your intent.
7. Be consistent—inconsistencies will damage customer confidence.
8. Adjust with changing times—whether driven by your actions or your competition's.

CHAPTER SIX

Brand Affinity

As elephants embark on their daily treks to forage for food, the herd often breaks up into multiple pods or small groups that wander off into the bush. Elephants consume several hundred pounds of foliage in a day. Spreading out this way allows every member of the herd to eat their fill without creating too much competition among the herd. In the dry season, the larger bulls and matriarchs will push over trees that would stop a full-sized, four-door sedan dead in its tracks to get at the green leaves that would otherwise be out of reach. On this particular day, one small group was led by a large matriarch to an almost-dry streambed. As they approached stream, they found themselves face-to-face with a large pride of lions, resting in the shade of an acacia tree on the bank.

Instantly, every elephant, large and small, raised their trunks and lifted their heads to face the new threat. Even the elephants that had not yet emerged from the bush to see the big cats were on alert. Lions normally avoid elephants—the king of the jungle has no quarrel with these giant pachyderms that could do major damage to a lion. After all, an adult lion looks quite puny next to a 10,000 pound elephant. Elephants learn that mock charges usually cause lions to run away and so this was the behavior the large matriarch adopted in this instance. These lions, however, were backed-up against water, which they also prefer to avoid. The lions did not run away and resorted to very loud growling and snarling and hissing and even mock charges of their own. This confused the elephants, but they did not back down, so a stand-off began. The tension in the dry African heat was extreme.

Within just a few minutes, two more groups or pods of elephants that had wandered four miles away from the larger herd arrived in a thundering cloud of dust and their large matriarchs joined the fray. Finally, the lions were overwhelmed by all this firepower and took to the water to make their escape. The elephants trumpeted loudly and charged into the stream to celebrate driving the lions away and take a cool, refreshing break. How did the elephants all know at exactly the same time where the danger was? How did the other pods, four miles away, know to come running to the aid of the group facing the lions? These behaviors puzzled human beings for a long time until research revealed that elephants communicate with each other at ultra-low frequencies below the spectrum that can be heard by humans and many other animals. These signals can reach over six miles across the savanna and apparently are clear enough to communicate intelligence to each member of the herd allowing the pods to roam for miles and yet maintain their connection with the larger herd. This powerful communication mechanism serves as an important vehicle in keeping the herd together, fed, protected from danger, and in constant contact—a unique form of affinity among the members of the herd.

The ultimate goal of effective brand affinity is to build loyal, unique, long-term relationships with your customers that make it very difficult for them to imagine switching to another vendor. Your customers should believe they belong to a unique club or association where they occupy a special position, and they are somehow enhanced by that relationship. They need to believe that your company and your people are integral to their operations and daily activities in meaningful ways, such that the distinction between "their people" and "your people" is blurred. Ultimately, you want them to be raving fans of your business.

Align with your customers

Where do you focus to establish brand affinity? Many will choose to focus in the marketplace, looking at other vendors and competitors to determine what might be appropriate for vendors in their market. Looking at the competition is useful to help determine how your business can be different. However, a far more effective model is to match your identity with your customers.

To secure long-term relationships and a sense of community with your customer base is to position your competitors as one of the many on the outside, making their efforts to displace you much more difficult. The customer's loyalty to your company will be a bonding agent so strong that even a well-performing competitor offering a similar service at lower price will find it nearly impossible to pry your customer away.

In the consumer world, a great example of this is the Harley Owner's Group (HOG). HOG members can't claim to belong to a club of the most technologically advanced, or highest performing, or most reliable motorcycles. In fact, they are less likely to define their relationship with HOG in terms of their bikes, than they are to define it in terms of their experiences: the rides, the rallies, their HOG member friends, and so on. Yet the common thread tying it all together is this undying devotion to Harley Davidson motorcycles and the spirit of freedom that they represent. They all dress alike, and they all seem to know each other on the highway with waves and nods of acknowledgment and assistance on the road or even just an impromptu conversation at a roadside diner.

These people are raving fans of Harley and HOG. The result? Harley Davidson motorcycles sell at a premium and are often backordered, with long waiting periods for delivery, despite their adequate performance, moderate technological features, and so-so reliability. The basic question for business to business companies is how can you create raving fans and that same sense of loyalty with your customers that Harley has achieved with HOG? The answer is not an easy one. You may not have a tangible product, and you probably don't have the ability for users of your product to form natural and casual communities where they would interact on a regular basis.

Let's take a closer look at this word sffinity. A dictionary definition is as follows: "Identification—a natural liking for or inclination toward somebody or something, or a feeling of identification with somebody or something. Connection—a similarity or likeness that connects persons or things." In other words, to create brand affinity with your customer is to establish a connection with them whereby they develop a natural inclination towards you and a familiarity that connects them with your business and your people. As discussed previously, to turn your customers into raving fans of your business, you need to become raving fans of them. That means you need to know them well, understand not only their individual needs, but understand what ties them together in their communities. What common identifiable elements exist in their environments that can be adopted as part of your brand strategy?

Everything from your brand identity, to communication style, messages and positioning, customer service, and the extra things you do to enhance the customer experience (which we will go into later), should have elements of affinity built into them. The goal is to become integrated with the customer's identity of themselves, who they choose to be connected with, who they rely on for their own accomplishments, and who they trust when making important decisions. In addition, which networks—formal and informal—facilitate the flow of information to them?

We will examine the range of elements that should be built into a plan for developing and executing a brand strategy. We will also provide examples of how affinity dimensions can be added to each element to assure that your brand strategy goes beyond simply aligning all your internal processes and functions with your brand promise. This approach to generating affinity can create a strong glue that binds your customers to your business for the long-term.

The scope of plans and processes needed to define and implement effective brand strategy is very broad. The plan and strategy must be endorsed and visibly supported by the CEO, who should hold all of his executive team accountable for its development, implementation, and continued execution. While a marketing officer may be assigned to lead and coordinate the overall effort, it can only succeed if it is integrated with the expectations and objectives every executive must meet. At the executive level, the key results indicators that monitor key measures of performance need to be consistent with, or have explicit metrics for, the brand promise.

The HR executive has a huge role to play, collaborating with the marketing officer, in evolving the employee culture to one that effectively delivers on the unified brand promise. Performance management, reward and recognition systems, training and development, recruiting processes, and internal communications all need to reflect the brand promise. This is a process where the CEO and the entire executive team must visibly support the brand promise through sustained efforts over a long period of time. Operations executives must ensure that their processes deliver results that can be measured against the brand promise. Internal metrics on efficiency and process improvement are critical, but ultimately, if the process that is delivering a service to a customer is not consistent with the brand promise, then the customer experience will not match what the internal metrics are saying.

Customer service must ensure that it delivers the experience that customers expect from the brand promise across every facet of this critical interface. Typically, when communication with customer service takes place, something has already gone wrong. The customer is reaching out for help. The experience with this contact, along with all previous and subsequent contacts, will become embedded in the customer's perception and weigh in on their assessment of your actual brand performance.

The Sales Department often begins the cycle by the impressions they create as they pitch the company and its capabilities and strengths. The message, style, personality and even method of delivery are all factors that need to convey the brand promise, so the prospect's experience with your company is consistent from the start. Finally, all of the market awareness, advertising, promotional campaigns, and literature managed and produced by the Marketing Department must be totally consistent with the brand promise.

The components, in different phases, will include: identity development, personality or culture, employee motivation including rewards and recognition, customer loyalty and satisfaction, sales prospect relationships, clarification of roles and expectations, communication plans (ongoing), performance measurement and management, and perhaps most important of all—affinity!

It's all about affinity with the customer:

1. Adopt elements common with customers
   - similar in nature or character
   - resemblance between persons or things
   - language, colors, symbols, behavior, etc.
2. Assure consistency in all communication
   - Marketing: sales collateral, promotional materials, advertising, web sites, trade show displays.
   - Operations: business cards, billing statements, products, packaging, reports
3. Integrate your identity with your customers
   - Secure long term relationships from the inside
   - Keep competitors out—create affinity hard to be replaced by pricing actions

CHAPTER SEVEN

BRAND IDENTITY

Elephant Identity

The elephant is clearly one of the great powerhouses of the animal kingdom. Often weighing in at more than 11,000 pounds, it is the largest of all land mammals.

An elephant's trunk is supported by 40,000 muscles and tendons. Strong enough to lift a large tree trunk, yet it is flexible enough to pick a delicate flower, elephants use their trunks for touching, grasping, lifting, tasting, spraying, smelling, and striking—oh yes, and breathing. A baby elephant will need at least two to three years of practice to become fully proficient at using this complex instrument.

Elephants' tusks are made of ivory. They are actually overgrown incisor teeth. Their tusks are important tools used to move objects, strip bark off trees to support their foraging efforts, and males use their tusks to establish dominance over other males. Elephants have very small eyes and their eyesight is poor. Yet they have an excellent sense of smell and hearing. Elephants will raise their trunks above their heads to sniff the breeze and discern what lies ahead. Their hearing is also highly developed and their huge ears can catch sounds at great distances. In addition, a hidden elephant talent is their ability to communicate at subsonic frequencies. These signals can easily cover 10 miles across the African bush, and they can communicate intentions and mood among other things that we humans do not yet fully understand.

As folklore has it, elephants have excellent memories. They are also credited with high intelligence. Elephants do have the largest brain of any mammal that has ever been measured. An elephant's brain can weigh as much as 11 pounds. When scientists measure the elephant's brain compared with the expected size of the brain for an animal of that size, they produce a ratio of 1.88. This means elephants brains are 1.88 times larger than expected for an animal of that size. By comparison, humans have a ratio in the 7.33 to 7.69 range. Chimpanzees are about 2.45 and pigs are 0.27.

Elephants can live up to 70 years in the wild. They are surprisingly good swimmers and can cover great distances across lakes and rivers, even in deep water. They need to cover a lot of ground because they eat for as much as 16 hours each day, consuming nearly 500 pounds of foliage.

Socially, elephants live in close communities led by a matriarch. As they forage for food each day, the herd will split up into smaller groups, each one of these led by a younger matriarch. Orphan baby elephants will often be adopted by an aunt matriarch in the herd, sometimes creating conflict with her own offspring. Adolescent male elephants are taught proper behavior under the direction and control of elder males. They usually are ready to leave the herd at the age of 12 to 15 years. In Southern African game reserves, male adolescents that were separated from their herds prematurely due to overpopulation issues went on a rampage and killed dozens of rhinoceros. When older adult males were reintroduced into the space, their behavior changed, and the killing stopped.

Clearly, this magnificent beast has a well-organized social structure and many powerful characteristics that make it truly the lord of the jungle.

How does the sum of your company's characteristics and brand identity measure up in your ability to lead a competitive marketplace?

Brand Identity

Several key elements make up the visual identity of the business. That is, those recognizable components that clearly distinguish your company from others and create a unique perception and relationship with the public. These brand identity elements include: your company name, logo, vision statement, color palette, fonts, and stylistic components that determine how the company 'looks' and 'feels' to others. The goal of brand identity can be expressed as follows: to make an indelible mark or impression on somebody or something. Indelible: impossible to remove. The greater the affinity your brand identity has with customers, the more difficult it will be for the customer to separate their association with you from their needs. This is the armor that will shield you from competitors and allow you to manage privileged and long-term relationships with your customers.

The challenge with existing companies is that there is already a certain brand equity attached to your name, sometimes wonderfully aligned with the brand promise and, often, not even close to what the company aspires to be. For new businesses, you are often compelled to create a name that is some morphed combination of words that result in a meaningless name that resembles an alien race on a science fiction show. The value of creating these unique names is that they are exclusive and can be clearly differentiated from other company names. The difficulty with such names is that they are meaningless and require a substantial investment in both money and time to create the brand image and communicate the meaning and purpose to the intended customer audience.

When the name Verizon first appeared on the scene, it had no particular meaning. It would have been a safe bet that almost nobody would have guessed that the name should be associated with wireless communications. After several years of brand development and advertising (recall the now famous "Can you hear me now?" line from their TV ads), the name is clearly known by consumers for what it is intended. In spite of this successful brand development effort, this is not a good example of a name that has natural brand affinity. In their case, the use of the tag line "Can you hear me now?" is a great example of how they connected with the consumer in a very meaningful way. Every cellular phone user can relate to an experience where their signal strength was not optimal, the call quality was poor, and they have asked the person on the other end of the call that exact question. This established instant affinity with the entire cell phone consumer market, and became a powerful mechanism for the company name making that connection. That strategy worked, albeit as a result of significant marketing investments.

Consider names like jetBlue® or MasterCard®: both are coined names but they convey a meaning that relates directly to what they do. In the case of MasterCard®, this name even implies something about the quality of the card in addition to communicating the card function: "master" of the cards. In the consumer's mind, this name is both meaningful and also creates a natural affinity. The consumer wants credit and debit cards, and if they can get them from the people who are "masters" of the card business, then they can belong to a special and unique group all privileged to have this distinction. This example illustrates how naming can create a direct connection between the purpose of the business and the consumer.

In business-to-business companies, the goal in naming is the same but the process is quite a bit more challenging as the nature of the business and its offerings is far more complex. However, having a name that aligns well with the intended business function and purpose and conveys direct meaning and value to customers is an extremely valuable asset. Such an asset will have a direct bearing on the size of the investment required over time to communicate and develop awareness in the marketplace. A name that is familiar to business customers in terms of financial services is Fidelity Investments. "Fidelity" connotes trustworthiness, dependability, reliability, commitment, devotion. The natural affinity is that this name communicates exactly what customers would want to experience in a financial services company that they are trusting with their money.

Everyone wants their financial services company to have those qualities, and if it's in the name, even better. In Fidelity's case, while they certainly need to deliver on these qualities to match the expectations of their customers, they don't need to spend much time or money clarifying what Fidelity stands for and the reputation it intends to earn. The challenge with using common English words, although they can be very meaningful, is that they are much more difficult to protect from a trademark point of view. If you are planning on creating a new name for your business, and potentially hiring one of the consulting companies that specialize in name development, you will most likely go down the path of comparing coined names versus descriptive names as well as considering morphed English words—assessing each possibility in terms of legal trademark registration, web URL registration, and internal management buy-in.

Whichever alternative you choose, the key quality you should look for in all of the research and analysis is whether the proposed names naturally contain any affinity elements that would immediately connect with your customers. As we demonstrated in the Verizon example, there are other elements, like tag lines, that can help you be successful. However, you will need to understand that you may need to invest more upfront to establish the name in the desired context. What if you could find a word that was commonly used by the customers in your industry? Perhaps this is a word that conveys a special meaning to insiders but does not have much meaning outside the industry. The naming consultants you hired advised against it because it didn't sound like a strong marketing name. Such a name deserves careful consideration, and it may be the key that creates an advantage through instantaneous affinity with your target customers. On the other hand, if your business dreams go beyond the narrow context of the meaning of this name, you may decide against it in favor of something that can be given the meaning you intend.

I recently came across an interesting example of just such a name: Purkinje, a medical software company. You're saying "Pur—what?!" When I first heard it, I had the classic marketing reaction, "What were they thinking?" It doesn't exactly roll of the tongue, it looks too complex, and my initial thought was nobody is going to know what it is supposed to mean. When I learned the meaning and relevance of the name, it became very clear and amazingly appropriate for the company's target market. According to Wikipedia, the online encyclopedia, Purkinje fibers are located in the inner ventricular walls of the heart, and they conduct an electrical stimulus or impulse that enables the heart to contract in a coordinated fashion. They were discovered in1839 by Jan Evangelista Purkinje, who gave them his name. Every physician knows the meaning of this word and the critical role that these fibers play in the functioning of the heart. The company has adopted a name that has a natural affinity from deep inside the industry that, in this case, is literally at the heart of their customer's business. While the name doesn't say anything about what the company does, it clearly places the company as a knowledgeable insider in the medical community—"one of us".

Many people are tempted to use descriptive names to communicate their business purpose clearly. While that approach does communicate the business purpose, it does nothing at all to connect the customer with your brand promise, and it does not allow you to stand out from your competition in any way. Take a name like Amy's Maternity Store. There's no mistaking what that business is about. It conjures up no special recognition from any other "XYZ" Maternity Store. However, I recently passed by a store sign that read "Ice Cream & Pickles Maternity Outfitters." Everyone knows the cliché about pregnant women craving ice cream and pickles. This name gives this store direct affinity with the experience of pregnant women. They have correctly recognized the importance of establishing a relationship with their clients and cleverly learned how to connect in a playful way with them by using this name. If the in-store experience reflects that same understanding and playful connection, they have a great chance of success.

Another risk with descriptive names is that people tend to reduce multiple words to acronyms rather quickly. So if you were very happy to be called Acme Financial Services because it seemed like a nice descriptive and meaningful name, don't be surprised to find customers and your own employees referring to your company as "AFS." What meaning does "AFS" convey? Not much at all unless you're an insider or already have a relationship with the company. Unless you plan to spend a lot of money to develop awareness for the brand "AFS" and develop the meaning in the marketplace that you intend, you'd be better off either choosing a stronger coined name or working hard to ensure that your employees and customers alike refer to your company as Acme Financial Services. Your brand standards guide will indicate that informal contractions are permitted when referring to the company in conversation so long as the contraction is "Acme" and not "AFS".

Finding a name that adapts across regional, cultural and language boundaries is equally important. Will the name apply easily in other countries to allow you to truly establish a global brand? Sometimes a name that was very strong in one market needs to be adjusted or even changed completely for use in a different market. For example, in 2001, the Honda Motor Company was planning their introduction of their new small sedan, the Honda Fit into the European market. They chose the name Honda Fitta to give it more of a European sound. Unfortunately, in the Scandinavian languages used in Norway and Sweden, the word fitta is a crude term referring to female sex organs. The vehicle was rebranded Honda Jazz.

But what if you have an existing, well-established company, and you're not sure that your name conveys your brand promise or has any particular affinity with your customers—how do you position your company for the future? You will already have brand equity and perceptions that are tied to the experience your customers have enjoyed with your company over time. Before you begin communicating any new brand promise, it is essential that you conduct research to understand exactly what your name represents to your customers. Which attributes do customers and prospects associate with your company's business purpose, values, personality, reputation for service, alignment with the market and technological leadership?

You may discover your existing name has key strengths you can build upon as you embark on your re-branding initiative, but you will also likely find many elements that totally contradict your plans in molding customer perception.

Even if your name doesn't connect well with your brand promise or business purpose, you may find existing brand affinity as well as customer perceptions that align very well with your intended brand strategy. These elements should be built into the new brand strategy and reinforced. Once again, research should not only focus on what the name means in terms of your business or reputation, it should clearly assess whether customers draw any natural link—or affinity—between themselves and your business.

If your company name seems like a clear mismatch, you really have two options: pick a new name and invest in creating awareness with your customers, or try the Verizon approach and pick a tag line that has a strong affinity with your customers and promote your company using that tag line. Either way, in the case of a clear mismatch the way forward requires an investment.

Logo

Close in importance to the name is the visual image that communicates your brand. Most businesses create a special visual form or logotype of their company name to create a unique, distinctive, and memorable connection between customers and the company. The logotype is frequently accompanied by some form of graphic symbol or icon that is intended to establish a visual identity that is memorable and further enhance the impression on customers. Whether or not a symbol or icon is used by business-to-business companies is not too important. Yet, if used, the logotype and the symbol must align with the attributes of the brand promise. Imagine the name Fidelity Investments and then think what logotype would best represent a company that wants to be your trusted financial services provider. The logotype should be strong, bold, and progressive to reflect both forward thinking and dependability—and it is. What if the company had chosen a flowing, artistic, or even whimsical logotype style to perhaps connote friendliness or the fun spirit in which they would like to manage your money? The result would clearly be a serious departure from the trust and dependability implied by the name Fidelity. How many customers would trust their money to a financial services company that looked like a playhouse when their name said "Trust me."?

In some industries, a specific font or style of type may exist for historical or business reasons. For example, if you were the ACME Check Printing Company, at the bottom of each check you print is a series of numbers in a special font called magnetic ink character recognition (MICR, e.g., 123489). If the logotype for the word ACME was created using a modified version of this MICR font, there would be a direct visual connection between ACME and its primary business product. The logotype would have a direct affinity with anyone who ever wrote or received a check. Of course, if ACME's business was broader than check printing, then this approach may be limiting. The style connection does not necessarily need to be as explicit as in the ACME printing example. The style should fit well within the entire industry that your company serves, the type of business and the nature of the relationships that you want with your customers. A business specializing in arts supplies and tools should have a logotype style that appeals to artists and resembles artistic styles that are familiar to that audience. What if the arts supply store had a big blue striped "IBM®" symbol on it? If you can't find or create a font style that connects with existing industry and customer perceptions, then the design should focus on the brand promise, messages, and the experience that your company wants for its customers.

For business-to-business companies, having a symbol attached to your logo may be useful if your business delivers a tangible physical product that the customer sees every day. On the other hand, if your name and logotype are strong enough then such a symbol, or an icon, may be unnecessary and it may even create clutter in your communication efforts. The ultimate goal is to simplify and clarify the communication with your customers and prospects and establish a clear and unambiguous identity and connection with them. Sometimes a symbol is used to enhance or modify the logotype, such as a circle swooshing around the name, or in the case of Verizon, a bold "Z" with an extended tail in the name, plus an exaggerated "V" used as a checkmark symbol next to the logotype. In other cases, the symbol is designed as a stand-alone icon that accompanies the logotype and may be intended to establish a unique visual identity with your company or product. The symbol should be simple and communicate a clear message to either identify your business or to imply an attribute about your business that is important to your brand strategy. Some symbols appear to have been designed by committees where every participant contributed a component to the design. Complex symbols that include multiple elements in an attempt to communicate a "story" rather than simply identify your company or establish a visual relationship should be avoided. They are not memorable, and they will almost never communicate the message intended. The general public can't read the minutes of the committee meeting to understand what the symbol is supposed to communicate.

In the consumer world, the Nike® "swoosh" has achieved the enviable position of clearly identifying itself with Nike®—even without the word appearing near it—and at the same time communicating the "Just Do It" attitude that Nike® has successfully promoted. This is a rare accomplishment, and it can only be achieved after a substantial investment in advertising and promotions reaching to the millions of people who wear the logo on their apparel every day. Business-to-business firms can never hope to achieve that level of recognition and, for the most part, they don't need mass consumer recognition to be successful. If you must have an icon or symbol attached to your logo, wouldn't it be optimal to find a symbol that represents some physical element or easily recognizable item in the industry you serve? If you're a financial services company, a symbol that resembles money, growth, or trust would seem to be a good fit. A machine parts company could use a stylized gear, cog or some other familiar product. A shipping company could use symbols that imply movement or speed, packaging, or dependability. These are simply examples, of course, as many symbols could be used in any of those industries.

Consider the example of Purkinje, described earlier. A stylized heart symbol or a design reflecting a nerve center would make a visual connection with the meaning of the word, if they chose to adopt a symbol. In other words, the symbol must ideally have an affinity with your customers' business, so that they associate your company with their business directly. A word of caution: some symbols are highly overused, and even though they may seem highly appropriate for your business, you would be better served by not investing money to join a crowd from which you can't be differentiated. Your name and logotype would be far better tools for distinguishing your identity in that case. For example, there appear to be copious numbers of icons incorporating people in some form or the other across the human resources and health services industries.

Color

What is the color of money? In the US we sometimes refer to the dollar as the "greenback." It seems appropriate, then, that Fidelity Investments has chosen to feature the color green quite prominently in their brand identity. Imagine that example of the IBM logo appearing on the arts supply store. What if the stripes in the IBM logo were each a bright color representing all the colors in the rainbow? What if the "M" also served as an artist's cup holding a few paint brushes, each with a dab of brightly colored paint sticking up out of the cup? Would this version of the IBM logo on an arts supply store be more appropriate and appear more relevant to customers who are artists? The use of color is a very powerful tool for communicating and establishing brand affinity with your customers. Choose an approach of establishing affinity with customers, before hiring expensive consultants to prepare psychological profiles and conduct research on competitors. Likewise, this approach should guide the executives inside who decide to utilize colors that would make them feel good about the company, regardless of the connection with customers.

This orientation toward affinity may not be consistent with traditional methods regarding the meaning and psychological relationship people have with colors. The information for choosing the best color lies with your customers and within your industry, not in some analyst's head or a text book. I recently did some branding work at a leading human resource solutions and services company. I asked the company president how he would measure success one year into the future. He said that one primary goal of the branding effort was to make the company the "friend" of every HR manager. In other words, he was searching for affinity. Early on, I made some observations at a national trade show attended by thousands of HR professionals. I noticed a few interesting characteristics of HR managers. First, the vast majority of them are female. Second, when they are in an air conditioned environment, women are more likely than men to wear a sweater. Third, and most importantly, the most common color sweater they wore was a nice bright and friendly shade of blue. The color is close to periwinkle blue or French blue. I quickly found a standard blue color from the Pantone color charts that resembled this blue, yet proved to be bold, vibrant, and unique. Then, armed with my new PMS279 blue color swatches, I had logo samples developed and other items using this color and began some informal testing with female members of the company, including but not limited to their HR managers. The response was a unanimous and resounding "Yes!" as this color made the obvious connection with it's intended audience. The color was adopted by the company. In addition to this color being used as a theme across all branded elements, marketing communications, etc., we took the idea of being the HR manager's friend to another level. All employees supporting all of our trade shows wore shirts in the same shade of blue to match the customers' sweaters. The result was that customers were heard to remark on how friendly and approachable the employees of the company seemed to be. Affinity!

More recently, in a major branding effort for a large health care technology and information services company, I was once again challenged to find a new corporate color. Research showed that most of the providers and competitors had adopted some formal corporate shade of blue, with one or two red choices in the mix as well. Again, instead of wanting to appear like just another vendor, I went out to the marketplace and looked to customers for clues. One of the most common and highly recognizable items by almost everyone in the medical and health industry, including every consumer who has visited a health care provider, is the clothing cover known as *scrubs*. Scrubs are not only very common and highly recognizable, but they come in a few bright colors. Perhaps the most familiar and recognizable color is a particular shade of green, commonly known as *scrubs green*.

Here was a color that was almost ubiquitous in the health care industry, yet not one provider of business information products or services to that industry seemed to take advantage of that fact. I created a color palette using this green as the primary anchor color and began testing it for recognition. Without prompting, many of the people who saw the green instantly called out "Scrubs!". The second-most common response was, "That's a very cool color." This became the corporate color for the new brand. Two significant goals were achieved with this decision: first, affinity with customers, and second, a clear distinction between this company and all of its primary competitors. Imagine if several vendors send a newsletter to physician's office. Most have a blue or red banner, and then one arrives with a scrubs green banner across the front page. The office manager and other staff at the office will instantly recognize the scrubs green as something that is a part of their environment—they may even be wearing it!

WHY COLOR IS IMPORTANT:

1. It creates an instant visual connection with customers.
2. Color can differentiate you from others.
3. It can align with your product/service/vision.
4. Color can help to simplify communication about who you are.

Protecting Your Identity

Some names are easier to protect as a trademark than others, and some businesses may strategically choose not to have a trademarked name. For example, business names that use descriptive and common English language words are almost impossible to trademark and just as difficult to protect. If your business is called Mid-State Financial Services, then you are faced with a challenge in that all of these words are generic words and cannot become the domain of any corporate entity. If Mid-State Financial Services operates within a specific region, as the name implies, with offices and signs on their buildings, then this approach may indeed work well for that business. Similarly, Best Cleaners would not be too concerned about a trademark for their name as they depend on the sign with the word Cleaners to drive local traffic into their shop. On the other hand, if you want to create a unique nationally, or even internationally recognized brand name that clearly identifies your company, then you may want to create a coined name along the lines of Verizon, Accenture, Google, and so on.

Whichever naming strategy you choose, you may want to be sure that you can protect your name from copycats who try to feed off your success, or even just inadvertently create confusion through coincidental usage. If you want a trademarked name that is easy to protect, then there are a couple of key points to keep in mind. You can start by doing a preliminary search of US trademarked names and terms by visiting www.uspto.gov and searching the TESS database. This will help to identify any trademark conflicts that may exist at a national level. This search will not reveal any state or international trademarks. Nor will it identify any names already in use that are not trademarked. This is important because you may register a national trademark with the US government and find yourself unable to use that mark in a particular city or region of the country because of prior use rules. Find a good trademark attorney to conduct a complete search. This expense will be worth its weight in gold should your trade name be challenged down the road when your business is established and your identity is well known.

When registering your name, your first step should be to register the words in a standard type font, like Times Roman uppercase letters. Then you may add the words as they will appear in stylized font to represent your logo, plus the specific colors that are used, and any symbols that may be attached to the logo to complete the identity. This gives you the broadest possible protection. Otherwise, if you had only registered the logo in graphical form, someone else couldn't use the same words with a different style and graphics. The name itself is protected first. Many businesses choose to register trademarks for their slogans or tag lines as well. Since these are usually all plain English phrases, they will often need to be associated with the logo in order to be protected. Before you go to the trouble and expense of registering a trademark for a slogan, give some thought to how long that slogan will be used and its strategic connection with your business. If you believe the tag line is an expression of your company's vision, then it is a strategic element worth protecting. On the other hand, if the slogan is developed for a temporary promotional campaign, then there may not be any value in pursuing a trademark—unless of course you intend to use that slogan again and again in subsequent campaigns.

To secure your trademark registration, you will need to demonstrate usage of the trademark or the registration will be weak and possibly unenforceable. Prior use always trumps a trademark registration. Usage means demonstrating that the name and/or logo is in fact appearing on public promotional materials including advertising, products, web sites, marketing collateral, and so on. Business cards and office stationery don't count. This doesn't mean you need to rush out with marketing material before you are ready to launch your new name, but typically within a year of registering the name, usage must be demonstrated. Over time, keep samples and photographs of promotional materials filed by date and include the geographical distribution of this material. This evidence will be very helpful when fighting off a prior use claim by a challenger.

A good example of a prior use dispute was widely reported recently when Apple launched the iPhone. They first had to negotiate a settlement with Cisco who had previously registered that name in the US but, apparently, had not used or maintained that registration. Then when Apple wanted to introduce the iPhone in Canada, once again, they were forced to settle with a prior registrant in that country, this time with a company call Comwave Telecom Inc. Similarly, when Apple decided to be in the music business with the iPod and iTunes, they ran into the Apple Corp. company in the UK, that was established by the Beatles. Apple successfully negotiated a deal with Apple Corp. for the rights to the Apple name. Having a strong and well-known international brand name does not protect you from prior use disputes when you enter new markets with new products that are outside the context of your original industry. For Apple, that was largely the computer industry as they were originally known as Apple Computer Corp. They later evolved to Apple Inc. as they have expanded their scope into music, telephones, and other new product lines. Clearly, you should be planning ahead for the use of your names and logo and anticipating prior use issues. Just as importantly, you should stay constantly aware and alert for new market entrants, as well as big existing companies, who may attempt to challenge you as well.

Immediately upon first use of the name/logo, you should attach the small "TM" symbol next to your logo to indicate that this is a trademarked name. Typically this would appear something like this, "Acme™ Financial Services", assuming of course that Acme would have been available for a trademark. Only once your registration certificate is received from the US Patent and Trademark Office can you change that symbol to the familiar ® such as "Acme® Financial Services". This indicates that the name is in fact a registered trademark of the company. One more note on trademark references, sometimes service-based companies choose to use the symbol "SM" for Service Mark, next to their name instead of trademark. From the trademark registration point of view, this "SM" symbol serves the identical purpose of the "TM" symbol, so they are interchangeable. Both will be replaced by the ® symbol once the trademark registration process is complete.

Next to registering a trademark, copyright protection can be very important to your business. The good news is that you may not need to do any research or pay lawyers for registration services. All intellectual property, including every written document that your company produces for public consumption, needs to display a copyright notice reflecting your name, the copyright symbol, and the year in which it was created. For example, "Copyright © 2008 Acme Corporation. All rights reserved." is usually sufficient to protect your material. This is not necessary on internal memos, business letters, billing statements, etc.

If you have products, like songs, software, processes, and other materials that are licensed for a fee, then a stronger copyright protection that is registered with the US Patent and Trademark Office (USPTO) may be advantageous. In addition, you may have systems, methods or techniques used internally to serve outside customers, or products that have a specific look and feel or design characteristic that makes them uniquely identifiable in the marketplace. You may also wish to protect these with a registered copyright. Actual samples of these products need to be included in the copyright registration.

In 2007, the Gallup Corporation, well-known for its surveys and the Gallup Poll, lost a legal dispute with a company named Kenexa over the content of Gallup's employee survey product. Gallup claimed that Kenexa had literally copied the content to create their own surveys and sold them as their own. The court ruled that Gallup had failed to register this survey content with the USPTO, including an actual example of the material in question so their copyright claim was invalid. This litigation took four years settle. The cost to Gallup in both legal fees and, if their claims were correct, of Kenexa copying their material, the potential lost business is astronomical compared to the cost they would have incurred completing this simple procedure. What would it cost you if your intellectual property was used freely by your competitors?

CHAPTER EIGHT

LOOK AND FEEL

Before making a final decision on the look of your brand identity, you would be wise to examine all the ways in which your brand identity will be communicated to the marketplace: Consider things like sales and marketing collateral, promotional materials, advertising, business cards, stationery, web sites, product designs, packaging, trade show displays, software user interfaces, and so on. Adopt a design style and apply it consistently to each one of these areas. Be sure the company name and logo, graphical fonts and symbols are consistently recognizable. Color schemes should flow throughout. Customers will become familiar with the look and feel of each of these elements, and they will recognize them as part of the same company. In essence, the visible touch points and interfaces with your company will provide a consistent experience for your customer and build familiarity to enhance the instant recognition of your business and simplify the customer's relationship with you. The best designs will boldly display the company's official color and have a clean, open, uncluttered appearance. Thus the company logo becomes its prominent identifying component.

Many companies make the mistake of using very complex and cluttered marketing collateral and web site designs. They describe their products in laborious detail, including screen shots of software and detailed technical descriptions. The look and feel elements are derived from their internal perspective—labs, production, factory floor or executive offices. These companies have missed the point. The purpose of marketing communication in all its various forms is not about who you are. It is about your customers, and effectively establishing long term relationships with them. Marketing is not to be used as a teaching aid to educate customers on the fine points of your product. Instead, it should be all about your customers' needs and how you will meet them. That is, which specific benefits can they expect? Which problems will you solve? Why are you a better fit than other choices they may have? Your design style, look and feel, photography, and all other visual design elements should start with your customers' needs and preferences.

Who are they? What is their business style? Purpose? Desired outcomes? Look for symbols in your industry that you can adapt and create as design elements. The symbol need not be a precise replica, but the resemblance should be obvious enough that customers will recognize it. Of course, it must also reflect your brand promise. Naturally, if your logotype, logo symbol, and color choice were already created with a view to achieving the optimal affinity with customers, then you have a significant head start on this process and can build on these elements to complete your design style.

Consider complementary design elements you can use to enhance and expand your basic logo identity that you can adapt and use flexibly across the entire range of communication vehicles. Let's say your business delivers software that automates functions and improves the efficiency of physician offices. You might learn from interviews that the most important thing physicians want from your software is to reduce time spent managing business administration tasks. They naturally expect the software to be accurate, easy to use, and to integrate well, across all facets of their practice. Your marketing literature, newsletters and web site can all include elements in their style design that are oriented toward this notion of successfully making administrative tasks more accurate and efficient, freeing them to see more patients.

Include elements in the design that are familiar to the physician in the course of attending to patients—not in the context of business administration. That is what the physician wants you to do. Your materials ought to focus on allowing the physicians to do what they want to do. Screen shots of your software, people answering the phone at your contact center, software design elements, are all totally out of place and will fail to connect with the customer. Your goal is to link directly with your customer's desired outcome and establish an affinity with that goal. Using your software, the physician can spend less time being a manager and be a more effective doctor. This way, you are also communicating that you understand their business needs and that you are committed to their success.

To connect to your customers, identify their desired results AND how those benefits will add value for their customers. Also understand how they share good results with others. Physicians want patients to be satisfied that they received the best possible care, and as a result have achieved all the positive benefit of their treatment. If your design elements and photography reflect happy patient outcomes then you will appeal to—or have affinity with—a primary goal of the physician.

Brand Portability

Your brand identity and the attributes that your customers recognize may be strong within the community of your customers and your local industry. Brand portability refers to the idea of using brand identity to launch into new markets, create new products or even break into new industries. With this type of move, there is the risk of altering the perceived value of the current brand and its strong associations with your existing products. The brand can only be transferred successfully to another market or product if the attributes and value propositions of that brand remain intact.

Let's examine an example to illustrate. Almost every major construction project begins with moving dirt. One of the most common sights on the work site is some very large yellow machinery. Very often, boldly painted on the side of these machines is the word "CAT" for Caterpillar®. For many people, the name "Caterpillar®" is almost synonymous with "bulldozer," and the big yellow machines are their icon. This is without any doubt awesome, heavy duty branding.

Now imagine if Caterpillar® decided, as some of the automobile manufacturers have done, to put their brand name on a mountain bike. Can you imagine what this mountain bike would look like, and what characteristics it might have? The frame would most likely be painted bright yellow with a wide cross-bar on which is printed "CAT" in big black letters. The frame might be made of lightweight alloys to keep the bike light and easy to handle, but the tubular framing would most likely be oversized and deliberately solid and large in appearance. All gears, cogs, and levers would also appear over-sized and extra heavy duty. You also probably imagine this to be an exceedingly rugged, mountain-traversing machine. With the name CAT on it, and the attributes you associate with a Caterpillar®, you will come to expect that this bike is an awesome, ultimate mountain traversing machine.

Now imagine a bicycle made by Porsche®. Would it be like the CAT mountain bike or would it instead be a silver, sleek, lightweight, road racing machine? Would the frame be slim and the gears and cogs also all appear to be fine, lightweight, and streamlined to glide through the air? Why would it be different than the CAT bike? The answer is that you associate the CAT and Porsche® brands with specific attributes that define your expectations for what these products are and how they function. Those attributes also establish affinity with the customers who buy and use their products. These examples illustrate that brand affinity can be extended into new products and new markets as long as you stay true to your brand promise. The affinity that you develop with different types of customers in various markets may shift as you work to establish your connection with them. However, in every case you must remain true to your brand promise.

Personality

The visual identity is often all that people in the marketplace who are not your customers will ever see or know about your company. To bring the identity and brand promise to life requires that the company and the brand are reflected in the behavior of every employee. The brand promise is delivered through the personality—a culture that is consistent across the entire organization and throughout all levels of communication—internal and external. The personality and culture must support the brand promise your customers expect.

Many business to business companies focus almost exclusively on the transactional relationship they have with their customers. Almost all of their energy is spent in assuring optimal operational execution and product performance. Believing that their service has been commoditized has convinced them to treat their customer relationships the same way—a service of a low-priced commodity. No personality, no relationship, and no aspiration to provide anything of higher value to their customers.

Do most large corporations have a recognizable personality? Let's try an exercise to see if you can identify basic personality traits of some large, well known corporations. For each of the 10 names below, think about whether the company has a corporate personality that is traditional in a classic corporate style, or whether the personality is fun and edgy. Make a small pencil mark next to each choice below:

1. YouTube™: __traditional __fun	6. IBM®: __traditional __fun
2. Charles Schwab: __traditional __fun	7. USA Today®: __traditional __fun
3. Geico®: __traditional __fun	8. Apple®: __traditional __fun
4. Volkswagen: __traditional __fun	9. General Motors: __traditional __fun
5. Google™: __traditional __fun	10. eTrade®: __traditional __fun

The first interesting observation is that based purely on the names of these companies, you were most likely to correctly guess the perceived personality of each of them. You were not exposed to any graphics, advertising, or other promotional material for this exercise. The important point to remember here is that there is no right or wrong answer. All of these companies are successful and easily recognized. Yet the fact their personalities are so easily identifiable is the result of a deliberate strategy. After conducting this test with thousands of people across the US, the vast majority of people recognize these company personalities as follows: 1. f, 2. t, 3. f, 4. f, 5. f, 6. t, 7. t/f, 8. f, 9. t, 10. f. Note that only number 7, USA Today, typically rates equally between fun and traditional among large groups of respondents.

For many business service companies, customers may only rarely actually touch or experience the company's products directly. Often, the only time when you talk to the customer is when something goes wrong, and they call you. In these relationships, the customer's experience is being driven by many interactions which either you have chosen not to control or influence, or the interaction was initiated by some sort of a problem.

The customer may be basically satisfied with your product or service, but are they satisfied with you? Do they see you as a valuable contributor to their success? Do they believe you understand and care about their needs and that your focus is to address those needs to make them more successful? Do they turn to you for advice when new challenges and opportunities arise believing that you may be able to help overcome them? Too many businesses fail to recognize the importance of the human interaction between their employees and their customers over the lifetime of their customer relationships. At the root of influencing the style of all interactions with customers, the real objective should be to build a unique relationship with them. If your business service or product can easily be replaced by a lower-priced provider, you may need to investigate additional value-added products that can expand the reach or commitment your customers make to your company.

A more powerful solution can be found in the nature of the relationship between human beings—in your company and in theirs. Based on your core set of values and your brand promise, how do you want your employees to behave with customers? How do you want customers to experience the interactions with your people? Certainly all of the traditional attributes like professionalism, trustworthiness, reliability, and customer-focused are assumed. These are foundational requirements by everyone that is serving your industry. Does your company convey a particular personality in its brand promise, design, look and feel, and through the behavior of all of your employees? These attributes can be defined by terms like bold, approachable, formal, fun, caring, casual, conservative, serious, or energetic, among others. These attributes define the personality style that you would like your company to exhibit and by which your customer will experience their business relationship with you.

The best place to start is by analyzing the attitudes and attributes of the specific customers you serve to achieve a level of affinity with their existing style, assuming there is a dominant style for customers in your market. By focusing on your relationship with the customer, over and above the operational performance, you can establish a relationship that goes far deeper into the psyche and overall perception of your value to that customer. If you can create a unique personality that establishes a deeper connection with your customers, you will have created a significant barrier for any competitor. The customer would have to face the prospect of undoing an emotional connection to your business to get that service for a nickel less with your competitor. This loyalty buys you time to respond to your competitor's efforts.

Let's say you defined your personality as bold, approachable, casual, and solutions-oriented. How would your sales representatives conduct themselves when pitching new prospects? Would they wear dark blue pin striped suits with black brief cases armed with PowerPoint presentations? Would the presentation be a long, monotonous, scripted monologue? Would they assume they knew exactly what the prospect wanted? Would they force the prospect to wait until the end before asking any questions or engaging in a dialog? The answer should be "no" to all of these questions if your sales representatives are in fact behaving in a manner consistent with your brand personality. What would your marketing literature and your web site look like? What style of writing would be used in marketing materials? Would it be college graduate level formal English in a very business-like tone, or would the language be conversational, informal, and designed for any 8th grade reader to understand? Most likely, the answer is the latter. How would employees behave and dress at trade shows? At your customer service center, how do they answer the phone? What message and music is played when a customer is put on hold?

Your brand personality must show up both in all physical representations of your company as well as in the communication and behavior of every employee. Remember, the example of the HR services company earlier with the choice of a friendly blue color? Well, that company's brand standards guide defines their brand personality as bold, energetic, friendly, and playful. "Playful!?!" You might say, "But they are delivering a serious service that directly affects financial performance. How can they be playful?" Don't confuse excellent business operational performance with the behaviors and personality that defines the relationships between your employees and your customers. The HR services company retrained thousands of employees to be more open and friendly and to have fun at work—with each other and with their customers. Their salespeople did not use PowerPoint. Instead, they would use props, dress up in acting roles, and play puzzle games with their prospects. Engaging the customer in a fun interaction up-front is a very quick way to establish rapport and show that you are approachable. Humor disarms their natural "bozo alert" defenses and engages them in a friendly way.

Southwest Airlines has delivered industry-leading financial and operational performance, and customer satisfaction for years. You'll agree that a business who's primary responsibility is the safety of its customers is a very serious business. Yet the experience that their customers have with its employees is defined as fun, engaging, and casual. This attitude is quite evident across the whole range of employees that customers may contact. I'm not suggesting necessarily that your company personality should be built on this attitude of fun. Rather, I encourage you to think outside the box and be willing to consider attributes that may seem a little different than what you've seen to develop a unique relationship with your customer. The key is to define your brand personality and systematically implement the steps needed for the behavior of every employee to match it.

ELEPHANT WALK
PATRICK SMYTH

CHAPTER NINE

EMPLOYEE CULTURE

Many business leaders don't have a clue what the employee culture is in their company. Nor do they know why understanding employee culture is important. Employee culture impacts every aspect of your operation and your business' ability to perform.

Culture can be defined as the behaviors and tendencies that people exhibit in:

- The way they interact with each other and with customers. Your goal is to ensure they represent the values of the company and its vision and reinforce the experience you have promised your customers.

- The decisions they make as they conduct their work. These decisions should be consistent with your vision, brand strategy, and values to assure they achieve the results you promised.

- The way they collaborate and solve problems. If they are aligned they will be empowered to make decisions consistent with your direction, or you will find all decisions are escalated to you which slows progress and increases costs.

- How well they stand up to new challenges and overcome obstacles. This determines their ability to work through problems and stay on track with the vision, rather than coming to a standstill each time new challenges arise.

- How consistenltly they express their purpose and loyalty to a common cause. This reduces internal competition and increases focus on results.

- The value and meaning they derive from the work they do. Being linked to a higher purpose allows them to understand the impact of their collective work on the customers they serve and the overall vision of the company.

If these behaviors don't match up, or if they are inconsistent across groups inside the company, the result will be inconsistent customer experiences and, most likely, lots of infighting among departments, lower employee morale and lower customer satisfaction.

If the basic behaviors of your employee population are aligned with your brand promise, they will produce consistent results and customer experiences. To be empowered, employees must believe in their leaders and team members, in their purpose and mission, and in their ability to delight the customer. If they do not feel any cultural affinity or alignment of purpose with their leaders or team members, they will act in ways that strictly conform to the minutiae of the work goals you have laid out for them. Uncertainty breeds fear, and they will respond by making decisions that fit within the narrow confines of their own work domains and personal spheres of influence. They will not risk a confrontation with other people who may choose a different approach. Some environments require workers to manage demanding processes and work heads-down for hours on end. Companies like that may be successful in spite of a lack of cultural affinity across its population. However, even in those cases, a predominant culture of fear is likely to emerge. Employees will focus on meeting the letter of their performance requirements. They will not act on behalf of the broader company or collaborate with others to make continuous improvements that would benefit the company as it strives to deliver a unique, best-in-class customer experience.

EMPLOYEE CULTURE WILL DETERMINE THEIR:

1. Behavior with each other and customers
2. Decisions on appropriate conduct at work
3. Ability to collaborate and solve problems
4. Response to new challenges and obstacles
5. Sense of purpose and loyalty to common purpose/vision

If you are uncertain about the status of your company culture, first assess the existing culture across every employee segment in your company, from top to bottom. Several consulting firms specialize in the area of surveying, analyzing and reporting on employee culture and satisfaction. Modern, internet-based technologies enable these surveys to be conducted quickly, at low cost, and to produce almost instant data. Before deciding on any particular firm, you should have a clear understanding of their service and how it might fit into your overall plan for redefining your company's culture. You will also need to develop a clear view of your desired culture that matches your brand promise, so you can measure where you are now and what changes might be needed.

An experienced consulting firm can also provide a reasonable benchmark for your company to understand how your culture compares to other companies in your category and identify the correlation between culture gaps and business performance. In addition, you will need to develop a roadmap for implementing the changes to your employee culture. This is a long-term process and can easily take up to two years to realize the full benefits of the changes, depending on the size of your business.

When deciding on a consulting firm, first ask yourself whether you have sufficient expertise in-house to plan such a process and guide it through to conclusion. You may prefer that the consulting firm develop a roadmap with you and guide your company through the process. Perhaps they will develop and hand over a proposed strategy, and you will dedicate the appropriate resources to managing the change process. Choosing whether to outsource or to manage this project in-house will play a big role in determining which consulting firm will best suit your needs. In addition to experience in delivering effective surveys and analyses, a consulting firm offers a very important benefit: independent, objective observation. If your company has a disjointed, unbalanced, or even a toxic culture, then a report on employee behaviors and attitudes may be best delivered and received by everyone—executives included—from a neutral, independent party that has no stake in the outcome, no internal agenda, and no political "baggage." The unbiased observer can expose real issues without fear of reprisals.

Employees are far more likely to buy-in to the proposed changes if they perceive that the executive team is taking the proposals seriously, agreeing to make the same changes personally and acting as champions for the new culture. In addition to executive commitment, three other important strategies can be very useful in affecting change in employee culture and to help them appreciate their role in accomplishing and delivering on the brand promise of the company. They are: training and development, reward and recognition, and performance management processes.

Training and Development

When new employees join the company, or when employees are promoted or transferred internally to new positions, do you offer any training to orient the employee with the company and their new role? Such training can be immensely useful in clarifying your purpose, objectives, culture, and tools that are available to the employee to help them become productive quickly. The messages and personality of your culture can be embedded from the start of the employee's engagement, ensuring they start off in the right direction. Perhaps you offer skills-based and technical training programs to your customer support and sales staff. Do you use that training to make sure the brand promise and culture of your company is communicated clearly and boldly? Do you routinely have senior executives participate in training sessions to welcome new employees and to provide their own perspectives on the company and its purpose and culture? Even if your training courses are computer-based and self-paced, appropriate messages can be integrated from top management to provide executive endorsement and a personal connection with the employees. People generally come to training courses with an open mind, expecting to learn something new—take advantage of that open-minded attitude and positively reinforce your brand promise.

Reward and Recognition

I recently worked at a company that had a multi-tiered recognition system. It started with a quarterly award in which employees could be nominated by other employees for taking action that was believed to be outstanding, and perhaps above and beyond the call of duty. The winners would be selected at the senior manager's discretion. Those who earned the most nominations in a year were eligible (assuming that other management and objectives performance measures added up) to participate in the annual President's Club trip. This prestigious affair was intended to include only the top five percent of the employee population below the executive level. This program was very popular within some departments, and the company literally spent thousands of dollars each quarter on cash and desktop mementos for this program. Unfortunately, they missed a significant opportunity to align this recognition system with their brand promise. If the nomination forms and the senior management selection process were simply applied against a filter of the behaviors and outcomes related to the brand promise, the company could have easily made a huge impact on the employee culture. Employees would recognize accomplishments, and management would select winners, for actual performance based upon a set of criteria that define the desired behaviors and outcomes to promote the brand promise. The successful example of the award winners would serve as a remarkable positive reinforcement to communicate the positive aspects of change in ways that very few managers could.

This company made an additional error that undermined the effectiveness of this program. In many cases, managers in certain departments selected President's Club winners by a raffle-style lottery. An executive drew numbers out of a hat and, regardless of performance or behavior, these lucky few got to enjoy the special recognition with the other "top" performers in the company. This is a terrible waste of money and a serious loss of opportunity to reinforce the value of high performance and dedication to your brand promise, not to mention it removes prestige and pride as motivating factors for employee performance. Does your company recognize employees through awards and exclusive trips? Have you clearly assessed how employees are selected and what messages are being delivered to employees through that process?

Performance Management Processes

Many companies are successfully tying salary planning and bonus allocations to individual employee performance, in addition to the company's overall performance. To make this a truly effective tool in aligning performance with your brand promise, you need to ensure that performance objectives, expected outcomes, measurement criteria, appraisal reviews, and the desired behaviors are all aligned with your brand promise, purpose, mission, and the desired employee culture. This is a very powerful mechanism for demonstrating your commitment and communicating your expectations to your employees.

If your company emphasizes teamwork and collaboration as a core value of your culture, you should reward those employees who have exemplified a collaborative spirit. This means work units, objective setting, performance measures, periodic project reviews and performance evaluation processes all need to be aligned with this principle of teamwork. Likewise, your core vision, values and other brand promise concepts must also be integrated with your performance and reward systems in the same way. A study released in 2002 by Watson Wyatt, an industry leading human resource consulting firm, revealed that "'Inspiration and values' is the most important of the six drivers in our Engaged Performance model. Inspirational leadership is the ultimate perk. In its absence, [it] is unlikely to engage employees." Your vision, values, and leadership demonstrated through a visible commitment and consistent communications are the most important elements you can use to enroll your employees in your brand promise and your vision.

TOOLS FOR ALIGNING EMPLOYEE PERFORMANCE:

1. YOU must 'be it'
   - Employees will mimic your behavior first, not your words
   - Frequent, direct, face to face communication

2. Recruiting
   - Select people who align with your vision/values

3. Training and development
   - New hire training/orientation

4. Reward and recognition
   - Incentives focused on achievements that exemplify brand/vision

5. Performance management processes
   - Objectives, measurements, advancement, linked with vision

---

CHAPTER TEN

Product Planning

As the team settled down for the night, the first sentry took his post. The sky was cloudy. It was the blackest of nights and the clouds made the air damp and cool. We were happy to be warmly wrapped up in our sleeping bags. Slowly, each man began to drift off to sleep under the watchful eye of the guard on duty.

At about the time when sound sleep should take over and pleasant dreams begin, a loud crackling noise crashed through the camp. Trees were leveled and branches broken as if they were twigs. Each soldier jumped out of his sleeping bag. The low rumbling breathing noise was unmistakable. Our camp had been invaded by a large elephant.

In the pitch dark of night, it was almost impossible to discern exactly the direction of the sound. There was another crash, this time a little louder and closer. Clearly we needed to mobilize quickly, but in which direction? Even a few seconds of indecision increased the feelings of heart-pounding panic. As section leader, I initiated our flight, moving through the thick bush, the rest following very closely behind, so nobody would be lost. Every few minutes I would pause to listen for the advancing elephant. It was still there and still close and definitely following us.

With its superior sense of smell, this was no contest. The elephant knew exactly where we were. On the other hand, we could not see or smell the elephant. All we could go by was the noise it made when crashing through the trees, and it was difficult to determine the direction of the sound. We crossed a clearing in the trees, and I took another look back. I could see that the once pale grassy area of the clearing was now a filled with the huge, dark mass of a bull. He was now just yards behind us.

With no other recourse, we broke into a run, bashing our way through tall grass, brush, and tree branches. For over an hour, this cat and mouse game continued. Finally, we came to a small rocky hillock and climbed up onto it. There we caught our breath and waited and listened. At last, the large pachyderm had apparently exhausted its curiosity, and with a loud trumpet blast turned way and wondered off into the bush.

Under normal night time conditions, with the benefit of sight, we would have been able to evade the elephant's pursuit with much greater efficiency and ease. You may think you can outsmart and outmaneuver your competition. Do you really know how well you will perform when your weaknesses are exposed through changing conditions?

Structure in the context of brand strategy refers not only to the organizational design and functional operations, but expands broadly to include decision making processes, target customer segments, go-to market strategies, product lines, product and service naming, distribution channels, and partnerships. Do your target customer segments match your brand promise? You may be selling to the wrong customer group, or not matching the correct customer group. The old "build it and they will come" strategy often does not work. You may find yourself with a host of product solutions that are a mismatch to customer needs. Are you trying to fit a product into a market because it seems like an obvious opportunity rather than understanding the needs of that market and developing a solution that fits?

Aligning with your customers extends to include your distribution channels and alliance partners. Are they the correct partners for your brand strategy? Each one of these partners will have an impact on your reputation, your products or services, and the manner in which you conduct business. The car dealer that services your car has a direct effect on your perception of the manufacturer. If the dealer is sloppy, slow or disrespectful, you will most likely transfer those impressions to the manufacturer as well. How are your channels and partners impacting your customers' impressions of your business?

Consider your product or service portfolio. Many managers are confused about the difference between a product, a service, or a solution. In the grand scheme of things, the current distinctions may be arbitrary and the discussion one of semantics more than substance. What you offer to customers for a fee is the product of your business. It may be a solution to a specific business problem or process, and it may, in fact, be delivered as a service, rather than a physical product. It is important to clarify how you sell and service the product that your customers buy and how well that product or service aligns with their needs and with your brand strategy. Business-to-business service companies often try to optimize their revenue opportunity by maintaining a strong separation between their product or service lines, believing that if each is sold separately then they can potentially extract more money. Then they might offer discounts for packaging additional products. However, this strategy can backfire as each component is a new product sale. If the additional products are not well integrated with the other products (or perceived that way), then it potentially introduces a new set of decision makers—slowing the sales process.

Sometimes businesses are driven by their product development teams, rather than their customers' needs and brand promise. Ask your sales, service, and support teams to tell you what really bothers them the most about the way your company launches new products. Are your salespeople frequently being asked to pre-sell products before they exist? You may be selling a product that you absolutely have to offer in order to compete, but there's no clear positioning message to help sales articulate why someone should buy it from your company. Does your hotline support team complain that the same general problems show up repeatedly with new products? Ideally, they should be able to successfully resolve the customers' calls within the first couple of months after a new product is launched. Do your implementation service technicians spend a lot of time gathering requirements for customized versions of your product, tailored to meet their customer's unique needs? Did your operations or IT organization team create a special task force that meets every Tuesday to determine how to support any new product announcements that have happened in the last week?

If the answer to any of these questions is "yes," you may be wasting huge amounts of money in poor sales performance, larger than expected service and support costs, and out-of-control operations or information technology infrastructure. You may be frustrated with each of these areas without recognizing the source of the problem. Let's say you were planning to open a new department store, attached to a large shopping mall. You, your architect and the construction company successfully put a building in the right place. When the doors opened on the first day, visitors entered the nice wide double doors and found there was nobody waiting to greet them. There was no store directory. After searching for the right department and finding the items they needed, they found the customer service desk and cash registers unmanned. The escalator to the next floor was all the way in the back of the building down a narrow hallway passed the restrooms. The entrance from the mall on the second floor was completely obscured by an artistic architectural design that displayed your logo up in lights. Not one person in the store had been trained on how to deal with returns, in-store financing, or helping customers navigate the wide array of products in all those different departments. The ladies' shoe department was on the second floor right next to the men's shoe department, and the cosmetics department was in a corner next to the coffee stand. Amidst this confusing layout, where was everyone? They were upstairs in a conference room meeting to figure out what to do with the scuba gear that arrived in the middle of winter in Minnesota.

How would those first shoppers describe their experience in this store? The likelihood that they would tell their friends to visit this store, or return to shop there again is extremely low. How do your customers experience your product and your company? Your engineering team may be very talented, smart and innovative. However, they must include all of the functional units that will be required to sell, service, and support the product in the process of planning, justifying investment, and developing new products from concept to launch. If they don't, you will more than likely be creating a long-term expensive mess—costing substantial time and money to correct, risking your reputation and hindering sales as well. Your top-line will suffer from difficulty in selling and your bottom-line will suffer from both poor sales and inefficient operations and service. Meanwhile, you will have to divert time and resources to correct mistakes that could have been avoided completely.

When designing your products or services to meet your customer's needs, you should include all your company's customer-facing groups in that process. Create a well-defined process, so they can participate and contribute to new product development. Once the product is launched, all of these customer-facing groups need to support the products in sales, implementation, hotline support and so on. Their experience in servicing your existing customers and products should have a significant influence on the design requirements for any new product. You may develop a phased process for managing the development of new products with explicit executive approval required after each phase to proceed with the next phase. It may look something like this:

Phase 1: New idea or concept evaluation
Is this idea really worth pursuing? Does it fit with your strategy? Does it enhance your existing product line and customer relationships? Will it clear the financial hurdles?

Phase 2: Business Case development

A thorough assessment of the market opportunity, competitive landscape, market functional requirements, required resources and timeframes, and detailed financial analysis including cost and revenue estimates for the entire lifecycle, or up to 5 years, of the product.

Phase 3: Design and develop specifications

Design and evaluate detailed specifications, engineering resources and schedules to validate the feasibility of the plan.

Phase 4: Development

Design the product and write the code, quality assurance through customer testing, implementation and support-service documentation and training.

Phase 5: Launch

Organization readiness including sales kits, promotional plans, pricing, final updated business case, and sales plans.

Phase 6: Life cycle maintenance and support

Customer service, support, software updates, service and satisfaction reports.

You may delegate the management of processes like these to product or business development managers, or even engineering managers who take full responsibility for driving a new product from concept to market. Make sure that they are not the only people—aside from executive review—who participate. The right time to engage sales, service and support, and operations in new product plans is Phase 2, the business case phase. They should validate market assumptions, evaluate functional needs to improve serviceability, and provide cost estimates to develop, launch and support the product. They need to sign-off on the business case at this phase to assure all requirements have been addressed. Then they should be fully engaged during the design, development and launch phases to ensure all needs are addressed during development of the product itself. At the same time, they should also be developing the tools, training, systems, and plans necessary to launch and support the product. Their sign-off on Phase 5, the launch, indicates they are satisfied that the product is ready and that teams are ready to sell, service, and support the product.

Engaging these teams in this way will go a long way to assuring that your products meet market needs and live up to your customers' expectations. This will maximize your ability to sell and provide support at the same time, thereby moving more quickly to profit. So, stop the weekly emergency meetings where your support services group is scrambling to handle unwelcome "surprises" from your engineering team. Instead, invite those teams into the planning process, and you'll all arrive at the same place together at the same time—what a concept!

CHAPTER ELEVEN

Product Naming

Several key factors need to be considered with regard to product naming. They include:

1. Was your brand identity created initially for the sale of one product? If so, evaluate the brand equity attached to that first product rather than the broader brand equity attached to your company. Can you expand, overcome or leverage that existing brand name? Most likely, your customers will know you by the name of that product, more than the name of your company.

2. If you are a business-to-business company, evaluate the customer's requirement for integration of workflow and information between services or products. This will clarify the need for integrated solutions and services under a single brand, versus separate products serving different needs with different buyers.

3. Evaluate the degree to which your product or service is specialized to address a unique set of needs in the market in a more-or-less

stand-alone fashion versus being a component of a broader solution. Your solution may need to integrate with other products and solutions from outside providers.

4. Evaluate the potential revenue to be gained and your ability to retain a customer who has purchased multiple products or services to address a broader array of needs.

5. Examine the degree to which any of your core product offerings are under severe pricing pressure and commoditization in the marketplace. You may need to consider expanding your product line and services to increase perceived value with your customers.

How you structure your product line and how you name it are all influenced by these issues. Do you sell stand-alone products or integrated solutions? Perhaps your company grew by acquisition and your portfolio includes legacy products that you have not integrated or renamed because you have been convinced that their strength lies in their brand identity and ability to continue to operate separately. Is that why you justified the acquisition in the first place, or was it to integrate the solutions into your portfolio? This is a common issue with companies that have grown by acquisition. Very often, the long-term strategy and needs of the customer seem to take a back seat to the interests of the managers inside the company.

Let's revisit our friends at the Acme Financial Services Company that we discussed earlier. They sell a collection of software products, information services and internet technology generally designed to address the financial and accounting processes of their clients. These services are sold in a modular fashion and are all designed to work together to provide a complete accounting and financial management solution. They include: general ledger, accounts receivable, accounts payable, treasury, cash management, tax filings, billing, budgeting and reporting. A customer may buy the Acme general ledger system, or any combination of products that meet their needs. If these different components integrate well and enable automation between processes, information and reporting, then the value and benefits of the complete set to a customer is far greater than any individual product.

Recognizing this, Acme decided that the optimal relationship with a customer is one where the customer buys most or all of the Acme solution set. Acme's key relationship with the customers is to provide financial services solutions. Their product naming strategy reflects this approach. They used a completely descriptive name for all of their products, each name attached to the Acme company name. Thus, Acme Financial Services became the meaningful collective name for everything they represent to the marketplace. Their accounts payable solution is called Acme Accounts Payable, general ledger is Acme General Ledger, and billing is Acme Billing, and so on. In this way, the product name says exactly what it is designed to do using the language that the customer uses for that function.

Most importantly, the name Acme precedes every product name so that the association with the products and services are continually driven back to the brand. The goal in this instance is to build the brand equity and establish long term loyal and trusted relationships with customers and the Acme Financial Services company, regardless of how the product portfolio may evolve over time, In fact, using this approach is more likely to ensure that the product portfolio will evolve in a way that aligns with the changing needs of customers. The customer associates the broader concept of financial services solutions with the Acme brand rather than any one product.

Let's contrast this for a minute with a different version of the Acme Financial Services Company. Imagine that Acme had grown through acquisition. Their original core product was an accounting package that specialized in general ledger, accounts receivable, and accounts payable processes. These products were sold as a product suite under the brand name "Fistar", so the Acme Financial Services Company sold a product called "Fistar GL" for general ledger, "Fistar AP" for accounts payable, and "Fistar AR" for accounts receivable. Every one of their 15,000 customers had bought Fistar GL and the other products had achieved approximately 50% penetration of that base. The general awareness and brand equity that customers had with the Acme Company was attached to the Fistar product that they had been using, and their perception of the scope and capability of Acme was limited by that product relationship.

Acme recognized through increased competition and price pressure that their margins were being squeezed and their product portfolio was too narrow to compete. They went on an acquisition spree to add other components, each strong market players in their own niche, and their resulting portfolio looked something like this:

Fistar GL – general ledger

Fistar AP – accounts payable

Fistar AR – accounts receivable

Tresact – treasury and cash management

Upay – billing

Xpend – budgeting and expense management

FlashIT – reporting.

The brand awareness and equity of each of these products was clearly attached to the unique branded name and singular focus of that product. The Acme management team had been convinced that the risk of integrating and re-branding these products would be disruptive to the established individual brands and prevent them from realizing their potential. They went to market with this new product portfolio and cross-trained their sales people on all of the products as standalone entities with their own value propositions. So, when the Acme salesperson called on the customer who used Fistar GL as their primary product from Acme, the name Fistar was far more relevant to them as they used and "touched" that product every day. Even though the customer was aware of Acme, the customer recognized this salesperson as their Fistar representative. The salesperson would try to explain the new portfolio and its benefits and introduce a host of new names which were, by and large, meaningless to the customer. It might go something like this: "Hi, you know and use Fistar and we are very pleased to let you know we have added major new components to our product line to be a more complete solutions provider. Let me tell you about our newest offerings: Tresact, UPay, Xpend, and FlashIT…" The poor salesperson probably wouldn't get past the second name before the customer began dozing off…or became overwhelmed by the options.

In this model, the Acme Financial Company was engaged in a game called "buzzword bingo." It's as though Acme (and many companies actually do this) was playing a mystery game with their customers to keep them guessing about what they do, hoping that at some point they would get it and yell out "Bingo!" The result was confusion, and the challenge of selling new solutions to customers increased with each conversation as customers struggled to understand Acme's identity. Worse yet, salespeople rapidly retreated to selling what they knew and trusted to put bread on the table in the short term. Is this really how Acme wanted their customers to experience their relationship with the company?

Of course, Acme might have made another choice as well. What if the "Fistar" product brand name had already become synonymous in the marketplace with Financial Services software and solutions? It may have achieved this through its dominant market share and years of successful advertising and promotions and the strong reputation of the products for accuracy and reliability. In this scenario, very few customers were even aware of the Acme Company since their brand association was very strongly with the "Fistar" product. The company had even developed extensive distribution channels and created certified Fistar reseller and certified Fistar developer programs to further cement the brand identity of this product. Assume Acme still found itself in a fiercely competitive position with its core products and decided, as presented previously, to acquire additional components to expand its offerings and relevance to its customers. In this case, Acme might be wise to keep the Fistar name as its flagship brand and rename its newly acquired "Tresact, UPay, Xpend, and FlashIT" brands to conform to this name.

The risk of changing a name with such powerful brand recognition and equity is indeed great and the cost of developing an entirely new brand for the same set of products is substantial. Before deciding which way to go, Acme would need to consider the applicability or relevance of the brand to the future direction and scope of the business. One consideration would be whether the brand Fistar was broad enough to include the newly acquired components. Let's assume, for this scenario, that it was. If not, it would pose a serious obstacle in expanding their brand. They might also enhance their product naming strategy to augment the word Fistar with descriptive words for each solution, just as in the first example where the name Acme was primary. In this case, Fistar would become the primary brand name. For example: Fistar General Ledger, Fistar Billing, Fistar Reporting, and so on.

For business service companies like Acme Financial, their first strategy of renaming every product using descriptive English language was the best option. Clarifying what the product or service does with simple language will make it easier for your customer to understand you and it greatly simplifies the sales process. No more playing buzzword bingo. Instead, your sales people provide value-added elements to your customer's business processes and outcomes. Adopting plain English also allows you the flexibility to use words to enhance the meaning of your products to support the brand promise of your company.

PRODUCT NAMING:

1. Use the product name or descriptive language to describe the product. Your goal should be to say what's in the box, or say what you do.

2. Plain English language simplifies the sales process. Make it easy for your customer to understand your business and help your sales people focus on filling your customer needs—not playing 'buzzword bingo'.

3. Adopt language that supports your company vision and clarifies the messages that communicate your brand promise to your customers.

4. Evaluate individual product brands vs. your company brand. A single unifying brand lowers your investment in marketing and sales, rather than investing in multiple distinct brands. If any of your products are experiencing commoditization, they may benefit by association with a broad offering. If you have consumer products that are sold on a retail shelf, they may require unique brand names.

PART 3:

DEVELOP AND EXECUTE
THE PLAN

CHAPTER TWELVE

CHANGE FOR THE
SAKE OF CHANGE

Make no mistake if you and your company are questioning your brand strategy and your ability to support a new direction, then you face a gigantic process of change, inside and out. Before you start, have you thought through the need for the change? People resist change. Sometimes even the smallest change can have a huge impact on an organization. Maybe that's where the old adage, "If it ain't broke, don't fix it!" came from—a plea perhaps, not to tinker with something that will take people out of their comfort zone. At the other end, however, Tom Peters advocated, "If it ain't broke, fix it anyway." Unless you adopt a philosophy of continuous improvement with the intent of proactively responding to market changes, your business will get stale. Staying ahead of the competition often means radical change—even when things appear to be working well.

What change makes a difference? Is there a clear business purpose to the change or are you really just tinkering? Aside from death and taxes, the only certainty we can count on is change. Customers' needs change. Competitors produce new products. New technologies revolutionize business processes. Governments issue new regulations. Regardless of how stable and steady your business seems, if you do not respond to these changes, it can quickly become obsolete.

Leaders must maintain a close watch on all these factors and build a proactive change mindset into the company's routine operating processes. If employees understand the need for the changes, they will rally behind them. This is a process of continuous quality improvement. The goal is to accept progressive change as a normal operating style. We accept the need to change in order to respond to evolving market conditions. This means proactively launching new initiatives to capture or maintain market leadership.

Unfortunately, leaders can sometimes force a harmful type of change on their organizations. The effects are particularly bad where change is not part of the routine operating experience. This change appears to be only for the sake of change. Perhaps it is intended to solve internal conflicts and mis-communications, or perhaps to quash political ambitions.

Benjamin Franklin said,

> All human situations have their inconveniences. We feel those of the present but neither see nor feel those of the future; and hence we often make troublesome changes without amendment, and frequenstly for the worse.

Avoiding risk sometimes influences leaders to make radical changes to existing systems and processes. They want to appear to be driving proactive change to lead their business and their industry. They also fear to risk making real business improvements. Making changes to existing systems that may, in fact, be working well creates the appearance of proactively improving the business. They may believe they have taken the safer approach, but the disruption can be risky.

Leaving a legacy and creating a mark on the company can be a strong motivator for a leader to make changes. Let's say that everything is running smoothly. The business is achieving all of its financial and operational objectives. Work-life is routine and almost boring, it's so smooth. What should the leader do?

He thinks there must be some way to improve the current systems, processes, or customer service. Process improvements could potentially squeeze out more productivity and grow bottom line profitability. Despite excellent performance and maintenance changes already under way, the executive announces a radical overhaul of some key process, or, more dangerously, to the company brand.

The company's mission may call for continued expansion to reach more customers in more markets, or new solutions and services to existing customers. However, developing and launching new products or expanding into new markets can seem a risky proposition. New investments and new skills and resources will be required. This threatens the bottom line and the comfortable status quo. Leaders who are intent on avoiding risk would rather reap the benefits of the current successful smooth sailing by making internal changes that seem more manageable. After all, they don't want to rock the boat with shareholders.

Making changes that don't have a clearly beneficial objective will convince employees that the change is simply an executive ego trip. The result? Employees don't buy-in to the change. Motivation and morale decline rapidly. The organization becomes confused and disrupted—a place of chaos. Among the employees, there are mixed priorities and commitments. The leader is unable to convince them of the business merits of the change—or to answer their "what's in it for me?" questions. Productivity drops precipitously.

What are the vision and mission for the business? What are the long-term goals and objectives for the business? Is the business—regardless of current performance—accomplishing its long-term goals and mission? If not, then changes may be appropriate. If the answer is yes, then what will be the course of action? Focus on the big picture. The current high-performing business may just be the right engine needed to drive the innovation and expansion of products and/or markets. Tinkering will disrupt this engine, not only preventing that growth but destroying current performance as well.

Change Happens—Make it Good

Each day brings new opportunities and challenges to your business. As a leader, you have three options: going all out for new opportunities, meeting challenges head-on while they are still manageable, or doing nothing. In every case, explicit or not, you make a decision about how to deal with change. Making no decision is deciding to do nothing.

When new exciting opportunities come along that could catapult your business forward, you may believe you have more time and there is no immediate urgency. Often, no action is taken, not even to study the business potential for the opportunity. Why? Because to evaluate the opportunity, you must think outside of your comfort zone. You know change would be required, and everything is running smoothly right now, thank you.

When potentially difficult challenges loom, as with new opportunities, you may believe you have more time and there is no urgency. At first, the challenge seems small. You decide you can deal with it later. Again, you do not even evaluate the potential business impact of the challenge if left unchecked. Or, you may perceive the challenge to be gigantic, requiring a massive response including significant change and disruption. Is this too scary for you?

What happens if you hide your head in the sand and ignore these questions? Opportunities disappear, or your ability to participate is dramatically reduced and comes at higher cost. At best, your business stays on its current steady course. That is, of course, if challenges you have ignored are not already dragging your business down.

Challenges threaten to hurt business with higher costs and lower sales, or drain resources that reduce productivity and/or your ability to deal with opportunities effectively. What happens if you ignore them? They become crises. Aware as you might be of the need to make a decision, the longer the delay, the greater the pressure to make a decision. When the issue becomes a crisis, the odds of making a sensible, informed decision at that point are low. Most people do not manage crises well due to lack of planning or failing to take a proactive approach to dealing with challenges that created the crisis in the first place. Then, the knee-jerk reactions and blame games begin as the business is disrupted by the crisis.

Look back to 1829, when Martin Van Buren, Governor of New York, wrote a letter to US President Andrew Jackson. Van Buren was concerned that progressive change would result in a gloomy future:

> President Jackson, the canal system of this country is being threatened by the spread of railroads. We must preserve the canals for the following reasons:
> 1. If canal boats are supplanted by railroads, serious unemployment will result.
> 2. Boat builders would suffer, whip and harness makers would be left destitute.
> 3. Canal boats are absolutely essential to the defense of the United States.

He continued on, saying that people werc never intended to travel at such breakneck speeds with engines roaring, scaring mothers and children and flying across the country—at 15 mph!

Imagine if Van Buren could have foreseen the potential for New York as a major hub for imports and exports for the US and Europe. He would have seen a great port city from which goods are transported rapidly across the entire country, providing work for thousands of people in shipyards, train depots, import/export trading, financing, and so on.

Fortunately, that change did happen. Certainly, it was a disruption for the people and businesses supported by the canal system. However, the benefit to the US economy was staggering. And now those "threatening" high-speed trains have been joined by an even faster trucking and airline industry. Progress requires change-even dramatic change.

Why is it that even though we can see change coming from the very germ of a great idea or from the first hint of problems on the horizon, all too often we do nothing? For each change, there is an optimal time to pursue the opportunity or tackle the challenge. W. Edwards Deming said, "It is not necessary to change. Survival is not mandatory."

Perhaps the biggest problem in dealing with change is the fear of failure. When we desire success, we may develop long-term goals and business plans for charting our course forward. Yet, how many times have the assumptions you made about the market, competitors, customers, technology, or government regulations or the economy performed exactly as you predicted? How accurate are your projections from year to year?

These factors change with time. If we are to succeed, we must remain aware and make changes and adjustments in our own business to achieve our goals. If we do not change, failure is assured. The real concern for many is the fear that they will implement a change that hurts the business. But remember, leaving things alone will let external circumstances drive the conclusion.

Good leaders learn to anticipate opportunities and challenges and prepare to deal with or exploit them. The earlier you are aware of an impending event, the sooner you can analyze, plan, decide, and implement changes that will keep your businesses performing at its best.

Someone once said, "If we don't change, we'll end up where we're going." Do you know where that will be? The constant you need to hold on to is your vision and mission—the purpose for your business—and the principles for guiding the behavior of your people. Staying focused on vision, mission and values, you can enjoy any opportunity or meet any challenge with your entire organization intact and rallying around the change. Otherwise, you may not meet performance expectations, or worse, you may be out of options. Embrace change and recognize that your brand needs to evolve with your business strategy and the changes needed to respond to the marketplace and your customers.

A Day in the Life of a New Idea

What if you're at the beginning of your new business venture? You know you have a great idea, but before you can clarify your brand strategy, you need a clear vision, and you need to convince others who may be able to help you develop and launch your idea into a successful business. Howard Schultz tells the story about when he was struggling to turn his small coffee shop business into the unique and successful enterprise it now is. Faced with a desperate financial situation, his father-in-law sat him down and asked him to give up his "dream and hobby" and to get a "real job" to support his family. But Schultz could not let go of his dream. He knew that his idea would work. More determined than ever, he went on to build the most successful coffee shop business the world has known. Most likely, there is a Starbucks store near you. Schultz knew that if he created a pleasant place where people can relax and enjoy not only good coffee but the company of their friends, he would have winning formula. By focusing on the customer experience, the Starbucks brand has definitely lived up to that promise.

Arthur C. Clarke said, "New ideas pass through three periods: 1) It can't be done; 2) It probably can be done, but it's not worth doing; 3) I knew it was a good idea all along."

Sound familiar? What happens when you get that great idea that you know, in your heart, has the potential to be the breakthrough you've been searching for?

First, you are so excited you just have to start telling somebody. The most obvious place to start to share it is with friends and family. Naturally, they'll share your enthusiasm, and maybe even help you get it started, right? WRONG! Family members are great for adding to the mental obstacles identified in Mr. Clarke's process, and that is, "You can't do it." Yes, you. Why do they do this?

Sometimes, family members and close friends feel a need to protect you from yourself—or so they think. Your great idea can be hard for them to grasp at first. Your idea may be ambitious compared to anything else they know about you, or themselves. They remember you as the kid who fell of his bike or got into trouble with the teachers or some other childhood event. They would prefer that you stay in the safety of the little box they have you in right now. That way, nobody gets hurt or embarrassed (starting with themselves) by your crazy idea. But don't lose all hope just yet, as a famous classical composer said, "I can't understand why people are frightened of new ideas. I'm frightened of the old ones."

Assume, after the discouragement from your family, that you are still committed. You then reach out to business associates, advisors, and other "experts" in the field. Surely they will see the light and be more objective than your family was. Alfred North Whitehead queued up the first phase of the idea process for us by saying that every really great idea looks crazy at first. That's right, get ready to hear, "It can't be done". Or, how about, "It's been done before", or, "It's been tried before and failed, and therefore it will fail again" Aargh!! What's driving this response? For many, it is fear. For others, the new idea is beyond their current imagination. Does that make it a bad idea? Certainly not.

Sometimes the naysayer acts as if they are trying to help you by challenging your ability to bring the idea to life. They will throw up many smoke screens to veil their own uncertainty about something so risky. They will say things like, "If 'big bad companies' steal your idea, then what will you do?"

Listen to Howard Aiken, "Don't worry about people stealing an idea. If it's original, you will have to ram it down their throats."

Somewhere along the way in the journey of your idea, you may find those who validate the idea with scientific reasoning, or letters of intent to buy your new product, or recommendations from experts in the field. Now your idea has credibility! Or so you think. Don't think for a minute that the cynics will be persuaded by this new found wisdom, insight, and independent authority. That brings you to the next step in the idea process, "It probably can be done, but it's not worth doing." Their fear of failure and their tendency toward risk avoidance is so strong they will not allow themselves to see the potential. So they raise the bar by asking you to justify the value of the idea, assuming it succeeded.

Real cynics or skeptics will keep throwing up new hurdles no matter how many times you satisfy their objections. On the issue of fear, let's turn to Martin Luther King:

> The soft-minded man always fears change. He feels security in the status quo, and he has an almost morbid fear of the new. For him, the greatest pain is the pain of a new idea.

You must believe, however, that potential investors, partners, buyers, and supporters will all, over time, come around to your idea.

When you finally break through, don't be surprised to find all those friends, family members, and other cynics who were so sure that you and your idea were headed for disaster suddenly becoming the geniuses who were responsible for all this success. That's the last phase of the idea process, "I knew it was a good idea all along." Or, how about, "I knew he could do it all along," or, "Heck, I was the one who told him to keep going when he wanted to give it all up," or, "You know, I remember the day we came up with idea on my front porch." Now what? Give them all as much credit as they want. Thank them for their encouragement. They will be more charged up and your idea will gain more support. Better yet, they will respect you even more for it.

Every new idea faces these obstacles. People resist change, they fear the unknown, and they are comfortable in their safe little boxes. It takes a special commitment and dedication to an idea to doggedly overcome all the resistance that you will face as you explore your idea. Sound business ideas that have real potential can have many of the risks addressed by creating a solid vision and strategic plan, and aligning yourself with key people who will become champions of your dream. The ultimate driver, however, has to be you. Take Walt Disney's advice: "Get a good idea and stay with it. Dog it, and work at it until it's done right."

Clarify your vision and your brand promise and follow Mr. Disney's advice and Mr. Schultz's example: be relentless.

CHAPTER THIRTEEN

The Strategic Plan

In the Kalahari Desert, elephants can cover long distances in searing dry heat for an entire day without access to water. Some of the best nutrient rich foods favored by these elephants are not located in dry river beds or along the banks. Instead they are found higher up alongside hills and mountains quite some distance away. Yet, there on the side of a rocky mountain in the scorching midday sun, the elephant is spraying water over its ears to stay cool. As the water evaporates quickly in the sun, the cooling effect on the veins in the large umbrella-like ears helps to keep the animal from overheating. At this rate, the elephant will lose about one gallon of water per hour, so knowing where to find a water source at the end of the day is critical. Sometimes these elephants will cross 40 miles of desert and hot sandy dunes to reach the next watering hole.

But wait, how exactly did they get that water way out there on the side of the mountain? Amazingly enough, these elephants store water in a pouch in their mouths that they can access during the day. This water pouch does not interfere with their foraging and eating vast quantities of brush and foliage during the day. This clever feat of planning ahead to make sure they have sufficient resources to sustain them for their journey is a learned behavior passed down from their ancestors. Over time, they evolved solutions that allow them to survive in environments seemingly hostile to all life. A purposeful, well designed and executed planning and management process can allow human beings to run a business with such fine-tuned, instinct-like behavior.

Before embarking on a strategic brand planning process, let's summarize and establish the overarching goals of brand management.

1. Align your brand with your vision

- Focus your entire business on one compelling vision. If your business vision is not clear, or is no longer consistent with your intent, then this must be clarified before attempting to define your brand.

- Align objectives and performance measures. In addition to aligning the messages and communication aspects of the brand, employee performance and results also need to support the brand. Setting vision-oriented objectives allows employees to relate the work they do (and expected results) directly to your vision.

- Reward performance consistent with the brand promise. Put your money where your mouth is. That is, if you recognize and reward employees for performance that exemplifies accomplishments toward the brand promise, they will rapidly adjust their behavior accordingly.

2. Establish a unique connection with customers

- Be part of the customer's community rather than the vendor community. Work to align your identity, style, personality, and perhaps even your business model more closely with your customers. This is the surest way to differentiate yourself from your competitors and establish long-term loyal relationships.

- For example, the Harley Davidson Owners Group (HOG) members are fiercely loyal to Harley Davidson. Ask a HOG if he would give you his Harley in exchange for a free brand-new alternative from Japan. More than likely the answer is an emphatic "No way!" Why? The reason is that the HOG would have to give up his HOG identity which includes valued relationships with other HOGs and Harley Davidson. This intangible, emotional cost is much greater and deeper than the cost of the bike.

- If your want your customers to become raving fans of your business, first become raving fans of your customers.

3. Manage the customer experience

- Across every touch point with your business, be aware of all the various ways that customers experience or come into contact with your business and make sure the elements are consistent in every way possible.

- If you do this well, you will accrue relationship equity, which is critical when customers buy. Whether or not customers already have a relationship with you, if you have accrued positive relationship equity, or a predisposition to favor your company or its products, when the time comes for them to make a purchasing decision you will be at the top of their list. This is also a strong defense against economic or market fluctuations. When buying slows down, you want the few active buyers to turn to you.

- Relationship equity can also be thought of as the sum of all the experiences with every aspect of your company. Every experience from each element over time builds to form a lasting impression.

4. Adapt the brand for each employee group

- Allow natural organization filters to adapt the message to their role yet remain consistent with the brand. Each function, such as engineering, finance or sales, develops a style and language that is primarily driven by their vertical profession. Likewise, layers of management will interpret the brand not only from their functional point of view, but also in terms of their perception of the best way to communicate the message to their employees. Naturally, they will interpret your brand messages into the context of their functions and roles and they will express those messages using their own, filtered, language. The goal is to assist and support them in adapting your brand message to their functions and ensure their interpretations are consistent with your brand strategy. Then make sure the business leader frequently, consistently and relentlessly reinforces the corporate brand message into every communication or report to employees, customers and shareholders.

5. Leverage the brand to achieve your growth

- Consistency and alignment create efficient use of capital. Every part of your business or communication that is inconsistent with your brand promise will cost you money. The short-term costs are typically correcting errors and redoing work. The longer term costs of poor customer retention, lost loyalty and fewer referrals are far greater. When everything is aligned, more energy is focused on achieving your vision with less energy wasted on distractions.

The planning model for developing and executing your overall business strategy establishes the context for planning and effectively executing your company brand strategy. A comprehensive, high-level model may include the stages and elements found in figure 13.1 on the opposite page.

Figure 13.1 — Strategic planning model

Strategy	People	Structure	Practice	Measure
Purpose	Culture	Alignment	Employee communication	Objectives
Vision	Development	Investment	Customer communication	Sales/revenue
Mission	Recruiting	Purpose	Customer experience mgmt.	Profit/ROI
Values	Rewards	Decision-making	Operations	Efficiency
Identity	Recognition	Alliances	Customer service	Employee Satisfaction
Markets	Performace mgmt	Partners	Sales	Customer Satisfaction
Customers	Communication	Customers	Marketing	Awareness
Products	Leadership	Products	HR Practices	Loyalty
Channels		Channels	Finance	Continuous Improvement
			Product	

Since the brand is an integral part of your strategy, the planning for brand strategy should begin with this model and then weave the brand development processes onto it. Aligning your brand development processes with your strategic planning will help to ensure that your entire organization and all resources, processes, and management are aligned to achieve your business strategy goals and objectives. This will also help put in place measurements to ensure brand performance is an integral component of your strategic operations and management processes. This model clarifies the scope that a successful brand strategy should have in influencing and perhaps even defining every aspect of your business from top to bottom. The job of developing, implementing, and managing your brand strategy cannot be laid on the shoulders of any one person or group in your organization.

Developing the Brand

The brand-related development phases are:
1. Strategy: including research, purpose, messages, and products.
2. Identity development: including visual elements, product strategy/positioning, business systems, collateral, and standards.
3. Execution and communication: includes employees, customers, and market.
4. Measurements: includes awareness, customer perceptions, and refinement.

The Strategy phase sets the core foundation on which all subsequent creative development work and performance standards will be based. Completing the Strategy phase will define the core messages that will communicate the brand, including the vision, mission, value propositions, differentiation, guiding principles and values. These messages need to be evaluated for effectiveness and refined in the context of the customers and marketplace your business will serve. This evaluation should begin with basic research to understand the current reputation of the company and its competitors. In addition, the research will reveal clues to identity elements (look and feel, style and personality) that fit with the customers in your market, Key product-related actions to be addressed at this strategy stage include product name, company philosophy and architecture, trademarks, product positioning, market fit, product design and packaging. All of these elements are the core components that shape the creative development and communications phases.

The identity development phase is the creative stage where all the visual elements that represent the brand identity are fashioned. This includes adapting core messages to different groups as well as creating standards and guidelines for brand management and measuring the effectiveness of brand communication later on. Specific elements include:

- The Logo. Your logo may be a stylized version of your company name. You may also have accents like arrows, swooshes, or symbols embedded with that stylized name. In addition, you may decide to have a symbol that is used in conjunction with your logo, but may also appear on its own without the name. The Nike® swoosh is a good example of this. Whatever your choice, the goal is to create instant recognition through a consistent representation of your company name. Remember, simple uncluttered designs are easier to replicate and adapt consistently. Your name and logo will appear on all visual touch points: products, web site, marketing literature, advertising, building signs, business cards, business stationery, clothing, promotion items, and more. In the design phase, you should test your logo in a variety of these mediums to assure that it will, in fact, maintain a consistent look and produce the recognition you desire across the entire spectrum. Survey tools can be used to measure customer preferences and perceptions to see which example they like best and if their impressions match the image and essence you want communicate. For example, the elements of a Preference survey may include: best appearance, most unique, most noticeable, easiest to recognize, most positive, best fit with company tag line or vision, and best fit for industry category. For the survey on Perceptions, ask questions based on the personality, style, image, your company wants to communicate. An example might include a rating scale where respondents are asked to rate sample logos for the qualities you wish to project such as: modern, effective, bold, customer focused, professional, energetic, industry leader, trustworthy, worldwide, accountable, and innovative. The result will indicate which logo matches most closely with the expectations you wish to communicate. You may be surprised just how much meaning people will glean from your logo when they are asked in this organized way.

- Color Palette. Once you have selected the primary color that you believe will establish the right level of affinity between your brand promise and your customers, you will need to develop a complete color palette. While you may have one official identity color, you will encounter applications where that primary color will not work. For example, if your logo is royal blue and you will be printing on an item that is also blue there will not be sufficient contrast for this to be noticeable. You may need to choose a different color not only for the logo but also any other graphical elements like banners, flags, callouts, etc. Create a palette with a few optional "primary", or first tier, colors. Then add to those colors a secondary, less bold, set of colors that complement the first tier colors to be used as accents, highlights, etc. These colors will be used across a broad array of media ranging from simple business stationary to high-gloss brochures to product surfaces to video and computer displays. Replicating the color palette successfully across all those different vehicles can be challenging. Just in the area of paper printing alone, you will find variations in color caused by different types of paper, different printing instruments (ink jet, laser, off-set, etc), and different inks. You can avoid a lot of expense and simplify production by picking standard colors from a Pantone color chart as a first step. Even with that, it will take some time to get the palette to replicate itself correctly. Plan for making adjustments.

- Typography. The type font you select for all communications with the world outside your company can speak volumes about your business and your culture. Imagine your business issues official government regulation compliance guidelines to corporations for use by their finance departments. If that material showed up in a Comic Sans or Bradley Hand font, chances are nobody would consider this to be serious, reliable, material. A more traditional Times Roman font may be more appropriate. Likewise, a children's playhouse company that used a Times Roman font would create confusion as well. Equally confusing is if you use different fonts for different types of communication. This creates a disjointed impression in the minds of customers and they will struggle to identify written material from your company with your brand. Like color, type fonts need to replicate across of the whole spectrum of visual communications media. Sometimes fonts don't translate well from one software program to another, and you may need to select a font from the same family (Roman, Sans serif, Arial, etc) to correct the issue.

- Photography. Photographs can help to connect people directly to the experiences you want them to have with your business and the products you offer. If you choose to add photographs to marketing and sales collateral, print advertising, web sites, and so on, make sure that the style and image of the photographs matches your brand personality and reinforces the messages in the material. Pictures of people need to be demographically appropriate to your target customers and preferably shown in modes that are relevant to their environment, not yours. In addition to selecting appropriate content, the tone of the pictures in brightness, pitch, color schemes, etc, all need to match your brand theme.

- The Voice. Just as the visual elements of your brand need to be consistent, the tone or voice used in all written material must be consistent across all communication formats. Of course, that style does not apply to official business documents and legal filings. What we are referring to here are communications that are designed to promote or support the relationship with your customers in any way. What you say is important, but how you say it is just as vital and frequently overlooked. Consider that every written communication influences your customers' perception of your company. Think of the broad-range of ways that your customer may read something about your company: on your web site, in marketing literature, press releases, annual reports, customer service announcements, newsletters, support bulletins, and so on.

Communicating in a consistent style with consistent messages will have a significant long-term impact on your customer relationships, and whether they will continue to do business with you. Your writing style, as well as the content, should demonstrate customer-centric knowledge with a confident and passionate tone. Engage the reader by using an active voice that quickly communicates the product benefit. Use a conversational tone by employing short sentences. Highlight scenarios that tell a story about the reader's actual business environment. Eliminate long, descriptive passages, drawn-out sentences, and college-level vocabulary

Here are 10 ways to make your written communication more effective:

1. **Start with the vision** or brand promise for your company. What promise are you making to your customers in your vision statement? All written communications should emphasize your primary brand message. Your content should clearly articulate benefits to the customer that highlight how your company is working to achieve its vision.

2. **Mirror your customers**. Check with sales representatives who have a solid reputation in your company for their input. If the language and messages used by sales people in the field matches, or complements, the customer's communication style, your sales productivity should improve.

3. **Use concise copy**. Resist the urge to say everything all at once. Make it a policy to cut the amount of copy in product packaging and marketing. Focus on your three or four most important messages and anchor everything else to those. As former President Franklin Delano Roosevelt said, "Be sincere; be brief; be seated."

4. **Focus on benefits and solutions**. Clearly highlight the benefits that add real value and solve problems for customers. The tangible benefits are what sell for you and should be the focus of your communication. The features that simply describe your product or service can be covered in the lower profile elements of your sales collateral. If you're not sure what to emphasize, go back to those high performing sales people and ask them.

5. **Avoid writing a "how to" guide**. High profile business and marketing communication should not laboriously describe how a solution works or is used. Customers want to know quickly how you will benefit them or solve specific problems they face with your product or service. They are not interested to learn how they can solve the problem once they have bought your product.

6. **Leave your internal jargon out.** Common and direct language helps you clarify real benefits and solutions for the customer. For example, 'software' is not a real benefit or solution. Accurate and timely access to financial data is a feature. Money saved identifying and correcting financial leaks is a benefit. Use words that your customers use and real-world examples to illustrate their meaning.

7. **Match images to your message.** Screen shots and detailed technical product pictures serve almost no purpose in marketing. When you see an ad for gasoline, they don't show you the pumps or the refinery. When car companies promote their vehicles, they don't show you the inner-workings of the suspension or engine compartment. Focus your marketing images on the key benefits of your product and find an interesting way to communicate that message as the selling point.

8. **Get outside feedback.** Share your work with others outside your company for review and feedback before finalizing it. Getting different perspectives will help to assure that the material is "getting across" to your prospects and customers. Just because something has a particular meaning or is considered very funny to people inside the company, it does not necessarily mean it will make the same connection outside.

9. **Keep it simple.** Brief sentences and sentence fragments are easy to read. Using sentence fragments appears conversational and also makes it easier engage the reader. Correctly structured prose designed to impress your college English professor is simply not needed in marketing communication. John Kotter said, "Good communication does not mean that you have to speak in perfectly formed sentences and paragraphs. It isn't about slickness. Simple and clear go a long way."

10. **Stay true to your vision and mission.** At every opportunity, maintain a consistent message so the customer will be reminded again and again of the central promise of your vision and mission. This consistency allows you to build meaningful and sustaining brand equity with your customers. Furthermore, it builds relationship equity with everyone else. When the time comes for them to make a buying decision, they choose you.

Whose job is it to develop all of this communication? Not just the marketing department, surely. This responsibility is shared by everyone in the company from top to bottom who may write anything that a customer might see. A standard set of guidelines and practices can help them deliver the experience you promised. How consistent is your customers' perception across all the communication channels? If you have inconsistencies, your customers' experience with your company will be inconsistent. What you say and how you say it makes all the difference.

TEN STEPS TO EFFECTIVELY WRITING
FOR THE BRAND:

1. Start with the vision or brand promise for your company.
2. Mirror your customers.
3. Use concise copy.
4. Focus on benefits and solutions.
5. Avoid writing a "how to" guide.
6. Leave your internal jargon out.
7. Match images to your message.
8. Get outside feedback.
9. Keep it simple for clarity.
10. Stay true to your vision and mission.

The Product Package/Diagram

Consumer products bear the brunt of the load in representing the company's brand to its customers. Marketing communications and web site content for such products should include high resolution, professional quality photography and illustrations that show these products in their best light. Business to business companies, particularly software or service providers, should use a visual description of the product set including a high-level diagram. That is, a diagram that illustrates the various products and relationships between them or categories in which they fit. The goal is to leave an image in the mind of the reader that allows them to easily comprehend, remember and recognize your product set. Naturally, the physical product design and packaging need to convey the same brand identity as all of the rest of your marketing and business communication.

The Website: A window into your business.

What about the role of your website? You probably already know that your website is a very important window into your company. You may recognize that your website must convey the image you want to all visitors. You may even view your website as an important tool for selling products and generating leads. Have you really thought about the experience of visitors to your web site and whether it helps to build long term relationships with them? Or, is your site just window dressing, just a pretty page with no particular function at all? You may be running a business services company or a manufacturing company and you think that a website is only important to people who sell direct to consumers. If so, you'd be missing a great opportunity and probably not getting the best return for your investment in your website.

Before examining the top goals of any successful company website, let's take a quick visit to your local department store and compare the experiences. On this visit, your goal is to find the men's clothing section and buy a couple of blue shirts for your husband. As you enter through the inviting wide front doors you find yourself in the ladies' cosmetics section. In the aisles are well-dressed women who greet you and appeal to you to try a free sample of perfume, lipstick, or hand cream. By tempting you with the idea of getting a free sample, they want to engage you in a conversation, and to have you stay for a while. Why? They know that if they keep you for a while, you may look around at what else they have. Even if you turn up your nose and walk on by, you have been greeted in the aisle by a friendly lady offering you something for free—not a bad experience so far. As you approach the center of the store there is a directory listing next to a bank of escalators. They made it easy to find what you're looking for and they gave you the navigation means to get to your destination quickly. After a quick glance at the directory, you're on your way to find the shirts.

In just a few minutes you have landed on the second level and you recognize that you have arrived at the men's section. In the middle of the aisle is a display stand with various office toys, golf paraphernalia, and fun gadgets. These interesting and unexpected toys grab your attention so you stop and browse through the items, pick one up to examine it and spend some time hanging out in the aisle. After looking over these items, you're ready to move on. But wait, is there more? Do you notice how your first inclination is to look around to see if there is another display nearby with more toys and gadgets? Of course, there is another one, right along the wall on the other side of all those shirt racks. You have to walk through the shirts to get there, but your interest has been aroused, so off you go. Chances are that even if you had no intention of buying shirts today, you may still have been tempted to stop and browse these fun items. Once again, the goal is to get you to stop, spend some time with something that interests you, and while you are there you may just look around at the merchandise they want you to buy.

Finally, you picked up your two blue shirts and you've made it to the checkout counter. The clerk at the register announces that you could save 10% if you used one of the store's credit cards for this purchase. Interesting… you were already committed to buying the shirts at the advertised price, so they didn't need to give you any money back at this point. Of course, this discount offer is not really meant to get you to buy anything else today. It is designed to convince you that you have a relationship with this store and with that discount incentive you will be inclined to come back over and over again. The clerk might also ask you if you'd like to be on their email distribution list so you can read about new promotional offers and products from time to time. This is another very useful tool for forging a long-term relationship with you.

How interesting that a brick and mortar store selling everyday products to consumers can work so effectively to make every visit rewarding and also work so effectively to build long-term relationships with customers. Yet, so many business to business companies who depend on long-term relationships for the continued profitability and growth of their business do very little with their websites to help develop and manage such relationships.

This brings us to our top website goals:

1. **Make every visit rewarding**

   Make the home page inviting, uncluttered, and friendly to visitors. Include promotional offers, white papers, demos, productivity calculators, and primary research studies that are of interest to your prospective customers. All of these are examples of ways that can make a visit to your web site rewarding.

2. **Keep visitors in your site as long as possible**

   The more interesting and higher the value of the information available, the more time visitors will spend browsing your site. Along the way, visitors will learn a lot more about your company, your products, and how you can serve them. More importantly, the time spent on your website won't be used developing relationships with your competitors.

3. **Create mechanisms to entice them to come back often**

   Online newsletters, blog posts, special events, opt-in lists, news announcements, and other fresh, rewarding items will keep your site dynamic and interesting and therefore encourage people to visit it often. Static web pages that are never updated with new information will go stale quickly.

4. **Be clear and consistent in communicating your value proposition**
   Simple, clear layouts and navigation schemes work best. Don't make visitors wait for clever flash animation sequences to run through to find out what you do. Overusing graphic elements can reduce the opportunity to include relevant words that can be found by search engines. Incorporate language that your customers use when looking for information on the services you offer. This will increase the likelihood your site will be found and, more importantly, that your value proposition is easily understood.

Be consistent with your brand identity and positioning, so the experience of visitors to your web site matches the experience you want them to have when they do business with your company.

TOP GOALS OF AN EFFECTIVE WEB SITE PRESENCE:

1. Make every visit rewarding.
2. Keep visitors in your site as long as possible.
3. Create mechanisms to entice them to come back often.
4. Be clear and consistent in communicating your value proposition.

Business System

The business system refers to all aspects of the business cycle and operational materials that may be seen or heard by customers. This includes billing statements, shipping boxes, business stationery, customer service telephone process, technical support websites, call-on-hold messages and music, and any other collateral that is created to support communication with customers in the course of normal business operations. Are your logo, color schemes, look, feel and appearance designed in an ad hoc fashion rather than being aligned with specific brand identity standards?

If so, chances are your customers will fail to perceive a clear brand message from you. In addition, you're probably overspending on design services to create all those disparate materials.

Also remember to align all customer-facing employees. How do they greet and handle customer requests, interactions, and support issues? I recently heard a speaker refer to the front desk receptionist as The Director of First Impressions. Your receptionist is very often the first company representative that outsiders will contact face-to-face. If they don't greet visitors in a manner and style that is consistent with your brand expectations, then they are most likely lowering your brand equity. You've heard the expression "First impressions are lasting impressions." Get the relationship off on the wrong track and it can take a long time to correct, if ever. Moreover, a bad reception experience may reflect directly on you as the person who hired and trained that person.

Marketing Collateral (print and electronic)

This is typically the one area that most companies focus on almost exclusively for brand consistency. By now I'm sure you recognize that marketing collateral is only one small part of the equation. Still, in reality, new prospects often will receive folders containing brochures, data sheets, case studies and white papers first—before they have a relationship with any other aspect of your company. This creates their first impression and is the initial step in their brand experience with your company. This material needs to represent your company to the best degree possible in every way from accurately communicating the professionalism, value propositions, and benefits, to visually and graphically representing the brand and the experience you propose to offer the customer. Not only should this material all be consistent, but since it starts the brand relationship, you need to ensure that everything in the customer experience from this point on is consistent as well. This allows their initial impressions to be reinforced and the relationship to build without doubt or hesitation.

Signage

Outside every building and every reception area wherever your company operates is potentially a big draw to bring customers in—or you can have a sign that confuses or even pushes people away. Just as the receptionist is the director of first impressions, the signs on your buildings and in your lobby areas project your image to the outside world. These signs should be consistent at all your facilities, and they should clearly and boldly represent your brand identity.

Trade Shows

This is where both the collateral and human aspects of your brand come together for contact with customers, prospects, and often competitors. A trade show is one of the few places where prospects will be simultaneously exposed to the many of the different facets of your brand that we have discussed. They will see your signage on your booth displays, experience the level of ease in finding information, watch your product demonstrations, and, most importantly, they will interact with your people. Will your people be approachable, friendly, knowledgeable, professional, helpful, respectful and demonstrate they are good listeners? How are they dressed and how do they behave in the booth area? How do they greet visitors and attract visitors into the booth? Many companies will staff their trade show booths with a mix of sales, technical support, marketing and product management employees. Each staffer will have different perspectives and levels of expertise and their personal filters will create the potential for different messages being delivered to visitors. Pre-show preparation should include training on key messages and themes, and also developing specific, measurable objectives for the event. Be sure everyone on the floor bears some responsibility for making the event run smoothly and meeting the objectives. No pointing fingers or passing the buck, or they should not be there. A trade show can be the initial contact with key buyer decision-makers. Their impressions of all contacts with your employees, including those on the lower rungs of the organizational ladder, are crucial. Make sure your staff is properly prepared.

Standards

Many companies who hire outside agencies to develop their creative brand elements fail to document brand management standards that should be followed across the board for all activity where the brand may be represented. This contributes to inconsistencies in implementation and unnecessary expenditures as each new opportunity for creative design comes along and employees and agencies alike believe they need to create something new. A centralized brand management function, typically led by a chief marketing officer, is essential to streamline and align marketing and brand-related communications. This role should create and maintain a comprehensive brand standards guide.

Included in this guide should be explicit directions and specifications for each category, plus guidelines and examples on the correct way to use each element. It should include examples of incorrect usage as well. The guide should provide templates for things like PowerPoint presentations or printed materials and tools to assist people in deploying brand-consistent materials. This helps to assure consistency and also reduces the need to create new material from scratch. Create an internal web site for employees to use and provide electronic examples of templates, downloadable logos adapted for different applications, and other creative elements. Add fun items like computer wall paper and screen savers as well to help keep the brand visible.

A sample outline for a brand standards guide follows:

Table of Contents for Brand Standards Guide:
Color Palette—for all print and electronic applications
Photography
Brand Design Elements
Personality

Who is "ABC" Co.?—exactly how should the company name appear in written materials?

Press Release—boiler plate language that will appear at the bottom of every press release to describe what your company is all about.

Corporate Vision, Mission, Values

Positioning Statement—what do we do as a business?

Segment Positioning—messaging tuned to different customer segments.

Product Positioning Diagram

Voice—i.e. language style

E-mail Signatures

Typography—fonts for different applications

Paper Stock—quality of executive letters, statements, envelopes, etc.

Standards—Common words and phrases that are used in support of the busines value propositions

Corporate Language

Back Page—similar to press releases, the boiler paragraph that closes out every collateral item with a statement about who we are.

Naming Conventions—How to reference trademarked names and other product names; a complete product taxonomy.

Quick Reference

RFP Template

Logo Guidelines

Logo Formats for Diff. Programs

Specific Segment Logo Guidelines

Tagline

Stationery—Design of Business cards, Letterhead, envelopes

Signage

Brand Usage Samples

Color Matching/specs

Creative Toolkit

PPT Template
Wallpaper/Screensavers

Web Design Guide

As a supplement to your brand standards guide, create a web design guide to ensure your website is congruent with elements of your brand promise. Describe the key web design elements including the correct navigation scheme, imagery, and text, to name a few. This guide will continue to be useful later on when adding significant updates, enhancements, and new content. With the guide, you will deliver a consistent user experience, even if you work with multiple developers and applications.

The design guide should include:

- General Layout: Begin with a "wire frame" or sitemap which is basically a hierarchical diagram depicting the structure of the site from the home page on down. A simple wire frame example may look something like this:

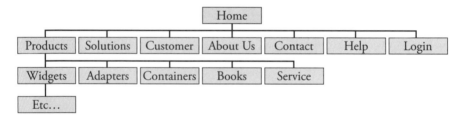

Next, outline design layout schemes of the web pages, starting again with the home page and subsequently plotting the landing pages, user input forms, and internal indexing. Ensure that all top-level pages can always be reached with one click of the mouse.

- Standard Branding Elements: Describe how the logo and other graphical elements are to be encoded and appear on web sites. Also include standards for other branding elements such as colors, font type styles, bullet icon forms, lines, arrows, and images.

- Variable Branding Elements: Indicate design standards for special promotional messages, sidebars, how to contact a representative, download prompts, and the style and use of pop-ups.

- Navigation: Define the style and placement of menu bars which may be at the top, left, in the body content, on sidebars, in footers, or login menus. Pages may include multiple locations. The goal is to make sure that each is used for a particular purpose and the rest of the site follows the same design style to keep the user experience consistent and ease navigation around the site(s).

CHAPTER FOURTEEN

Executing the Launch Plan

As you prepare to launch and execute a new brand strategy, your communications sequence should start from the inside and then move out. That is, the first audience for your new message should be your team of employees, executives, and close working partners/alliances. What would be the experience of a customer who heard your new brand message before your staff? Next, share your new brand with your existing customers. They have already invested in your business before the change, and you want to bring them along with you. Finally, your last communication phase should target the broader marketplace. As the message ripples out farther into the marketplace, be sure each ring supports the next. The timing of these different steps can be as quick as you can logistically manage while ensuring the integrity and consistency of the message. If you believe employees can absorb and correctly reflect the message within a day, then the customer communication can go out the very next day. There is no reason to delay for any set period of time.

Let's take a deeper look at each step in the launch communication sequence:

- **Step 1—Employees.** Your goal in this first stage is to make your employees effective ambassadors of your brand promise. Get them excited about the change and provide tools to help them communicate and represent the brand as you have designed it. Be sure you have their "buy-in" before you put them in front of customers.

  Be sure you communicate clearly the need for change. Help employees understand the big picture and how this change affects the whole company as well as specific divisions or work groups. Help employees stay forward focused to help ensure that your vision and brand promise are accomplished.

- **Step 2—Customers.** If your business has multiple customer segments that use different products or services, create a unique communication for each customer group. In addition, make sure that each sales and customer service representative also receives copies of the same communication, so they can help customers interpret what they have seen. As with employees, you want to create excitement among your customers and get them focused on your new brand promise.

  Explain the change in the context of the new expanded role you see for your company and show how this change will benefit them. Anticipate their questions and include a Frequently Asked Questions section with as many relevant answers as you can to provide as much clarification as possible on all aspects of the change and its impact.

- **Step 3—Market.** Once your employees, partners, and customers are aware of your new brand strategy, you can broaden your communications campaign to reach as many people in your target market as possible. Advertising and promotions will help create awareness of the company and its products and services. You may also include public relations and media interviews to generate press coverage. Focus on getting articles published in key publications that are either read by your target customers directly, or may reach potential partners. Your goal here is to jump-start a buzz in the marketplace for your business. This communication is designed to reach out far and wide. Search for cost-effective promotional campaigns with a strong call to action and Web-based viral marketing campaigns to create an almost immediate demand for your products.

ELEPHANT WALK
PATRICK SMYTH

CHAPTER FIFTEEN

COMMUNICATION

You've developed your communications plan to launch your business or your new brand. Who is accountable for executing the plan? You might say it's the Chief Marketing Officer. Not exactly: The responsibility rests with everyone in the company! Starting at the top, everyone must own, lead and be a champion of the brand stragegy. It must permeate all people and processes. The CEO may designate the Chief Marketing Officer (CMO) as the steward of the brand and program coordinator. In this role, the CMO collaborates with the senior executive team, manages developing the elements that will be used to communicate the brand strategy, and works in close partnership with the senior HR executive to align employee and recruiting policies with the brand strategies.

However, the overall responsibility for the successful implementation and performance of the brand strategy rests with the top executive team. It is they who must incorporate the brand strategy into their functional or operational units and ensure that each domain is appropriately aligned and thoroughly incorporated into their management processes. Further, employees and customers need to see and hear clearly articulated support, belief, and commitment to the brand strategy in all communication, formal or informal. Weekly staff meetings, team meetings, business updates, goal-setting, town hall meetings, newsletters, management operations reviews, performance evaluations, email messages, decision-making, and every other action must reinforce management's commitment to the brand.

The message here is that while formal communication mechanisms are a means to deliver prepared messages to employees, the more powerful communication is the result of everything you do in conducting your business, managing work, making decisions, and leading people. In other words, if you totally believe in and are committed to your brand promise, then you will reflect that commitment in the purposeful style in everything you do.

Aristotle said, "We are what we repeatedly do. Excellence, then, is not an act but a *habit*." For the brand promise and vision to become a habit, you must practice it in every aspect of your business life.

This same philosophy applies to customer communication. Remember that for customers of service businesses, every touch point, human interaction and advertisement forms their perceived experience with your company. Therefore, in the case of customer communication, it is even more critical that every employee consistently deliver the brand promise in the same familiar style across all customer touch points.

Drive Your Vision

Jack Welch, former chief executive of General Electric Corp., said "Good business leaders create a vision, articulate the vision, passionately own the vision, and relentlessly drive it to completion." Why do so many new business ventures start with such enthusiasm for a new idea, only to be resigned and deflated a short while later? It may be convenient to assume the product or service is simply not a good match for the market. That assumption would most likely prove to be just plain wrong.

You had a great idea for a new product or service, and you started selling it to anyone that would buy. Your business took off and one by one you picked up a sizeable customer list. You thought you were successful in chasing your dream. Then, after a couple of years, you find yourself stalled. After all these months, you seem to have hit a wall.

No matter how hard you work, you can't seem to break through. How do you make this business grow? What happened? Many new business leaders who reach this point react by taking on a micromanagement strategy. An over-controlling C-level executive severely restricts any sense of empowerment within the team who must execute the company vision.

Start with your attitude. Look at the habits you've adopted along the way. Adjust your attitude to separate your identity from your business vision, or dream. You [personally] are not your business. Realize you are simply the steward of your business vision and brand promise. You can then develop an objective and balanced perspective on the real potential of your business. From there you can determine which resources you need.

If you keep tying your sense of self and identity to your business, you will constantly create limitations on what you are willing, or believe you are able to do to pursue your dream. You will probably become over-controlling and inadvertently hamper its growth. Worse yet, you may become overwhelmed by your own vision as it expands in scope and size.

Before you begin the strategic planning process, develop a clear and objective vision for your business. This work is essential and perhaps the most important contribution from you as leader of the business. With a clear vision for the future, you can confidently begin planning. Establish long-term goals. Gain the commitment of key people inside and outside of your business. Plan activities and deliverables needed to accomplish the plan. Estimate the revenues, costs, resources, time, and capital needed to accomplish your vision. Define milestones to measure progress along the way. All strategic plan elements, combined with the customer-focused orientation discussed earlier, lays the foundation for planning your brand strategy.

The planning process includes short-term (up to 12 months out) and long-term planning. Having a clear vision allows the people you depend on to develop and execute each of these initiatives to align with a common purpose. Following these steps will simplify and clarify your vision and how it can be accomplished. Better yet, it greatly increases the potential for your success.

Use the mantra, "Big plans, little steps" as a constant reminder of the need to stay focused and committed to your vision. At the same time, stay equally focused and committed to the planning process required to achieve it. Re-examine your vision and strategic planning process each year. Constantly adjust your business as market and competitive forces change. You and your team will be able to apply every little step to take you just a little closer to realizing your vision.

You may succeed at directing and delegating the work required to accomplish your vision. However, the real key to successful execution is exemplified by the words Jack Welch used, "… passionately own the vision, and relentlessly drive it to completion." Your employees and other team members will observe and ultimately emulate your behavior, regardless of what you say.

Clearly demonstrate your vision and brand promise for your company directly and frequently to all team members. They will only commit to your vision and pursue it with passion if they see this passion and commitment in you first. Do not delegate this assignment and do not underestimate its importance. Take the big plans; little steps approach, and stay relentlessly focused on your vision. Then you and your entire team can drive your vision to successful completion.

Hiring Experts

Hiring experts to help guide you through the process of developing your strategic plan and your brand strategy can make a lot of sense. Appropriate experts can add tremendous value to your strategic plans and your ability to implement and manage your strategies effectively.

You should, however, choose the right type of expert at the right time. Unfortunately, many companies of all sizes and levels of sophistication make similar mistakes when they decide to embark on a strategic brand development process. The story often plays out as follows. The CEO realizes that the company needs to invest in developing a new brand identity. Someone in the company is "tagged" with the responsibility to figure out how to do it. Very quickly, the entire company becomes aware that they don't have the internal expertise to lead this effort. Even if the work is delegated to a Chief Marketing Officer or VP of Marketing, very often that person lacks the relevant expertise or experience to develop new corporate brands.

In order to demonstrate progress to the CEO, the CMO or other tagged leader hires a creative marketing agency to develop the brand. Of course, the CMO doesn't have sufficient expertise to make a thorough and meaningful evaluation of the agency. The agency's plan sounds very cool and dynamic, bold, exciting and energetic and the company gets swept up in the ether. Then the agency comes in and asks all sorts of questions about the company's strategy, vision, values, mission, value propositions, target customer segments, and so on. In other words, they are asking for all of the elements that should already be in the company's strategic plan—which should be the basis and foundation to guide their creative work. Since this is not available, the agency offers to conduct a study and lead a strategic planning workshop for the company's executive team, or simply design the strategic plan for them.

After a few weeks, the agency returns with five sample mock ups of advertisements to review with the management team to see if they are capturing the intent of the brand correctly. The first is one they believe will most closely and most conservatively match what they interpreted during their internal studies. The second is a more creative piece that is designed to stretch the imagination of the management team to see how they react. The third is an outside-the-box piece that would probably never be appropriate but is designed to break up a meeting that is starting to frustrate management and also see how far their emotional connection can be stretched. The fourth one is the secret weapon. The agency team members will be all excited with anticipation before they show this one to the team. This is the one their creative people like best and they really want the company to adopt. The fifth sample is a total throwaway purely for humor, so they can lighten up the room and help the management team have some fun with their brand.

The management team ultimately finds that none of the samples match their thinking very well but there are aspects to some of them that are worth exploring. So the agency records that feedback and plans to return in two weeks with another set of samples. This time, all five samples are more closely tuned to the target. As the selection process continues, management's frustration grows, and so do the invoices from the agency. Eventually, the company's budget is stretched to the limit, and the management team settles for whatever was last put on the table. Then the creative development and planning for the launch and marketing communications begin in earnest. The story ends when the company's new brand and promotional programs hit the media and they learn the hard way that it just is not connecting with customers.

Why does this happen? Mostly it happens because too many executives don't understand the important connection between their brand image and a solid, well-thought business strategy. As a result, they hire creative agencies that are not business experts—not the best qualified to develop your business strategy. The agency wants the money, so they'll say anything and even put forward what appear to be useful business processes for developing the strategy. Everyone rushes to produce something to get to the creative part of the brand development process. The agency makes a few educated guesses as to what might be the best strategy and hopes that something will stick. The company continues to pay the agency for their guesswork until either the budget is exhausted or the agency somehow manages to produce a winner. In the end, the company is not happy with the result or the agency, and the agency is convinced that the company simply does not have its act together. The ultimate cost to the company in rework, error correction, paying for guesswork, and lost opportunities is enormous.

This is not an indictment against creative service agencies. It is intended to point out the gaps in understanding and expertise that exist inside the company, with the management, and outside, with the creative agencies. When the business strategy is not properly developed beforehand, the hired agency does their best to fill in the gaps. The bottom-line is that strategic planning in the correct sequence is critical to being able to create and implement the new brand successfully and cost efficiently. Knowing what type of expert to hire and when will make a world of difference in saving time, money, and frustration.

Getting the expert sequencing right:

FIRST   Develop the business vision and strategy—a strategic planning expert can certainly guide you successfully through the process.

SECOND   Conduct your own research about how well the vision, mission, and values will connect with your customers and identify and define all of the affinity elements that are discussed in this book.

THIRD   Hire a creative agency that is capable of adapting their expertise to your business strategy and bringing the brand promise and all of the affinity characteristics to life.

CHAPTER SIXTEEN

THE FIRST 100 DAYS

The first one hundred days are critical to gaining momentum when implementing any significant change or new initiative, such as executing a brand launch plan. Why? The awareness of the need for change and the willingness to go along with the change is greatest when the concept is fresh and leaders demonstrate their enthusiastic support. This is the time to implement specific actionable plans and to require key players to become accountable for important elements of the plan's success. During this time, reiterate the brand promise and goals to your leadership team. You cannot over-communicate to them, no matter how frequent your interactions and how many times you feel you are repeating your messages. Likewise, require frequent reports on progress toward achieving key milestones, Even if some strategies won't be implemented until months later, it will serve to reinforce their commitment to the plan. This level of support will be evident to their peer group and help build the momentum.

In every organization there is a political culture that determines how things get done and by whom...and sometimes even what gets done! Corporate politicking is driven by a few individuals and their desire to have more control, and is perpetuated by co-conspirators who cooperate either out of greed or fear that their positions will be threatened if they don't.

When a new key leader joins the organization with a specific set of skills and talents and for a specific purpose—such as to re-brand the company, or to change the entire customer service orientation and infrastructure in the company, the initiative must quickly achieve a highly visible position as a mandate of the organization.

If the momentum on the project is not achieved and sustained in the first one hundred days, then the likelihood of its long-term success will be seriously diminished. The political network will slowly weave its web and alter components of the plan, shifting the priorities of the key stakeholders back to their familiar fear-based roles. The entire plan will slowly unravel. You may successfully implement superficial elements of the plan, such as changing your visual identity and the look and feel of your website and sales collateral, but the changes needed to shift the operational and behavioral DNA of the company to your brand strategy will not happen. When employees below the political saboteurs observe the behavior of their superiors, the dissension will grow like a cancer, and nothing more than lip service will be applied to implementing the new brand.

If you create a plan that involves all of the key leadership up-front, and require each of them to focus substantial energy toward achieving the re-branding program goals, then you will effectively re-shape the political fabric, and not allow anyone to undermine your plans. Stakeholders will be too busy demonstrating to the CEO and to each other that they are taking the necessary steps, and they will become champions of the change with their employees.

Holding regular weekly progress reviews for a few months, along with direct one-on-one meetings with the CEO and other key leaders will elevate the importance of the re-branding plan—for a while—above the agenda of the political network. After the hundred day period (or several months), when it is clear the program is being executed in a complete and thorough way, the frequency of review meetings can be reduced to monthly and even become integrated into normal business and operational reviews. Along the way, be sure to develop systems for employee reward and recognition as well as learning and development to guide and direct employee behavior towards your brand promise.

Delegating

Every business leader wants to achieve the best result and get the greatest return on investment. Experienced business leaders may be better qualified to undertake specific tasks than most of the people on the team. Presumably they attained their positions, at least in part, by rising up through the ranks through their outstanding performance and varied experience. Does that really make them the best person to do every job?

You have probably heard the old adage, "If you want it done right, do it yourself!" Perhaps you have even said it. I bet if you heard your boss say it, you didn't feel too motivated or empowered. This philosophy taken too far is not likely to build mutual trust. To demonstrate low confidence in the team's abilities will destroy any motivation that may have existed. How can anyone be expected to go all out and do their best when the boss's favorite tune is "Anything you can do, I can do better!"? How would such a boss respond to even a small mistake?

To be successful, a leader must learn to balance the desire to control the process with the need to empower the organization to perform at its peak. Great company leaders use their experience and expertise to direct, guide, advise, motivate, and nudge the organization toward expected objectives.

In sports, a good coach functions in the same way. While the coach sets game strategy and expectations for each player, he still has to trust his team to win the game on the field. A good coach learns to identify and exploit the unique talents and skills of each individual player. With expertise and guidance, a skillful coach molds the team and shapes it into a high performing engine. Team members performing at their full potential, each knowing what is required of them and how to work with the others, and all united to a common purpose will be empowered to make the best decisions and create optimal solutions to move forward. This powerful engine will drive the company toward its goals with seemingly unstoppable momentum.

Maintaining absolute control over every action and dictating how each process and milestone is to be achieved will not generate empowerment. Leaders must learn to trust the team. They must accept that the team will often choose their own approaches to solving problems or developing processes for managing projects. The leader needs to know when to step back and look at the bigger picture and decide how to motivate and empower the entire organization to support and accomplish the vision and mission of the company.

To brush team members aside and rush in to personally tackle the task directly will almost assuredly demoralize the entire team. They will neither feel respected for their abilities nor appreciated for anything they accomplish. The signal sent to the staff is that they are not good enough. They will lose motivation to put forward creative ideas to solve problems and move the business ahead with speed. Most likely, they will crawl into their defensive shells and try to avoid being noticed, lest their heads roll for having the audacity to make a decision or offer an out-of-the-box idea.

The reward for empowering the team and accepting new, uneasy solutions will be astounding. For every one of those uneasy solutions, more and more innovations will surface that never would have seen the light of day. The true creative power of the entire team will be unleashed. In this way, the unique talents and brainpower of each team member is allowed to develop and they can freely create without the constraints of fear.

Empowerment is what delegating is really all about. The coach does not delegate the job of defining the vision and mission and setting objectives for the team. The coach does, however, effectively delegate the job of each position on the team to the best player to execute that position.

Likewise, business leaders do not delegate the job of defining the vision and mission and setting expectations. Team members execute the actual work processes, projects, tasks, methods, and day-to-day activities required to accomplish the mission. The vision and mission becomes everyone's purpose—leader and team member alike—but each plays a unique role in accomplishing that mission.

Letting go of absolute control can be challenging, and it does sometimes require a leap of faith as accountability for specific tasks and processes is shifted to someone else. Start small. This is a process of retraining for both the leader and the team. With each small step, both will share more trust and acceptance and, over time, larger steps can be taken with confidence.

Small, detail-oriented tasks that were previously dictated in great detail and monitored can often be easily managed by someone else. Let staff decide what to do next and review their progress weekly. Agree on the expected outcomes, and let them get there. Of course, as a good coach would do, be sure to provide frequent encouragement, direction, guidance, and advice. Then enjoy the surprise as the team shows just how much they can accomplish.

Perhaps C. S. Lewis said it best:

> "It may be hard for an egg to turn into a bird: it would be a jolly sight harder for it to learn to fly while remaining an egg. We are like eggs at present. And you cannot go on indefinitely being just an ordinary, decent egg. We must be hatched or go bad."

The bird is fully-formed inside the confines of the egg's shell, yet it cannot fly until it is released. The bird first has to peck its way out of the shell before it can test its wings and fly. Leaders must similarly release their people from imposed restraints, so they can learn to fly. Focus everyone on the same vision and brand promise. Empower your staff to execute the steps to achieve that promise. Allow them to soar.

Listen and Lead

"No one ever listened themselves out of a job" —*Calvin Coolidge*

Have you noticed that we seem to devote a lot more time and effort in learning how to talk to people than we do learning how to listen to them? We are taught that to become effective leaders, we must be powerful orators able to deliver a speech, be heard, be understood, get a point across, persuade, entertain, engage, motivate, and more.

Hundreds, if not thousands, of books have been written on the subject of talking—several times more than there are telling you how to listen. Beyond the books are seminars, workshops, video-taped speech training, and on and on. All of them focused on how to be an effective speaker. Someone once said, "You have two ears and two eyes and only one mouth. Use them in that proportion." This is sage advice indeed. Why, then, do so many books emphasize exactly the opposite?

We seem to believe that effective leadership is defined as: force of will, delivered powerfully in impressive oratory fashion. Do that well enough and you will lead people anywhere you want to take them. Really? What kind of leadership is that? Do you want a wise leader, or simply a noisy leader? A noisy leader is so intent on dictating the conversation that they never listen. As a result, they never consider the needs and ideas of those being led.

If you want to be an effective speaker, wouldn't it make sense to know that you are connecting with your audience from their point of view? Henry Ford said, "If there is any great secret of success in life, it lies in the ability to put yourself in the other person's place and to see things from his point of view—as well as your own." Doesn't that imply that you ought to spend a great deal of time listening before you talk? Can a leader really learn much about the people they lead if they don't listen to them?

Leaders who struggle with delegation typically are so intent on telling people what to do and showing them how to do it that they are also weak listeners. If you are a noisy leader and feel compelled to micromanage, the best advice for you is to learn to change your language. That is, ask questions that serve to clarify intent, resolve misunderstandings, and overcome challenges. Ask questions that lead people in the direction you are proposing. Once you have asked your questions, wait for them to speak and listen to them. If this type of back-leading is done right, they may believe they arrived at a conclusion on their own. In fact, they did, because the conclusion was reached by asking questions and letting them express their thoughts and ideas. The idea here is not to coerce or manipulate them into doing something. Rather, it is a process of understanding their views and perspectives on an issue that you want them to deal with before dictating the next steps.

By asking open, non-judgmental questions, you will communicate clearly two things:

1. Your primary concern is to learn so that you can move the business forward productively.

2. That you care about their interests and needs and value their insights to help guide you and the company forward. When you show you care, they will care. People will believe that you care when you ask them questions. They will most certainly never care because you know the most or speak the loudest. If they believe you care, you will gain their trust.

If you're not accustomed to listening, give it a try sometime. Instead of announcing a surprise decision, ask your team what they think first. That conversation could go something like this: "The issue I'm determined to address is blah blah blah. The impact on us of this issue is blah blah blah. I'd like to hear your thoughts on this issue and how we can solve it." Then guide that conversation to consensus on:

a. Clarifying the issue

b. The impact of the issue on the business

c. One or more acceptable solutions

Then you are ready to make the decision with their full support and understanding.

A good clarifying question is one that encourages an open and insightful answer rather than leading people to a conclusion. Ask if they agree with your views on the issue and do they see any other impacts that you have missed. Ask what would be their preferred outcomes for the business in solving the issue. If they provide an answer that doesn't seem specific enough, simply ask them "Why?" and repeat until the specifics are clear.

In every case, make sure you give them time to think through the issue. Get them to be comfortable sharing their thoughts and then be patient enough to hear them all. You might just find that the path of empowering your team will be far more graceful than attempting to will them into submission. Why? Getting the team on board and aligned with the solution up front means that they can immediately and enthusiastically get into action.

One final thought: You must act in accordance with the chosen solution. It does you no good to talk about a solution and then behave a contradictory way. You will fool no one, and you will train your team to behave the same way. As Dr. Stephen Covey said, "You can't talk your way out of a situation you behave yourself into." This is particularly important advice if you are making strategic changes to your company's vision, brand promise and employee culture. To get your employees to willingly and enthusiastically come along with you to your desired outcomes, you must first understand their perspective.

Selling the Project

What if you have an established business and the change in your brand strategy would require a radical overhaul of your company's identity, processes, and employee culture? You may have several stakeholders that need to be convinced of the need and value of this change prior to launching your plans, in order to gain their support. Without this support, the change process will be undermined and potentially never reach its desired conclusion. The risk to your business of such a failure is very significant as it directly impacts your future growth potential. Identify the stakeholders in terms of funding sources including the executive team, board of directors, lead management team and key influential employees and key customer relationships.

One of the biggest contributors to resistance is too much focus on your self. Some ways that people sabotage themselves in selling stakeholders on change include:

- Putting your own needs ahead of your passion for the opportunity.

- Focusing on getting their commitment rather than presenting an opportunity to be successful through the higher purpose of your brand promise.

- Allowing your fear of rejection to curb your enthusiasm and confidence.

- Poorly thought logic for how you propose to implement changes and engage them in the process.

- Insufficient supporting information to validate your assertions.

- Denial about the magnitude of the change and inertia that already exists.

- Lack of understanding about the risks and failure to plan possible mitigation strategies.

The team will evaluate your communication based on how effectively you demonstrate the value of the outcome you are proposing. Is it desirable, achievable, and are you committed to seeing it through? This requires a balance of two key elements to be successful— that is, a balance between the vision, and you. Imagine a scale that must balance with the weight of the opportunity on one side and the weight of your commitment on the other.

On the opportunity side, you must convince them that the vision is worth pursuing. You understand the problem thoroughly. You have a clear and compelling long-term picture of what the outcome will be. You can identify a significant number of people who acknowledge their desire for the outcome you are proposing. You understand how to reach these people and get your solution to them. You are aware of the competitors and why your vision is a viable alternative. You have a clear, logical process and model to prove that this project will produce benefits to all involved. You have assembled a strong team of people to help you accomplish the project. You understand the key risks involved and have developed mitigating strategies.

On the "YOU" side; you must convince them that you believe in this vision and the outcome you seek to create. You are confident that the proposed project will be executed successfully and deliver the outcomes you are seeking. You are passionate about the vision and the potential that this project has to make the difference you believe is possible. You are committed and dedicated to achieving this regardless of the bumps in the road that will appear. You must believe without hesitation that this is the best solution, and that it will succeed. You must be courageous enough to present and defend your project to just about anyone, setting aside your own ego and fears.

Focusing on the opportunity side allows the magic to happen. Specifically, you need to address the following considerations:

- Build the case for why this is a great opportunity, how big it can be, and why the outcome is so compelling.

- Articulate your understanding of the changes and organizational resources that will be required.

- Demonstrate that you understand how to layout a roadmap to success.

- Illustrate the risks and challenges that this project will face.

- Outline the proposed actions to mitigate risks.

- Share the competency, experience, and overall ability of the team you have assembled to successfully execute the project.

- Convince them that you have thoroughly assessed the opportunity, and the risks and the resources needed.

- Show them that you understand the value of their commitment and how that commitment will be converted into success for the company and for them as well.

Now watch what automatically happens to the "YOU" side as you work on the opportunity side:

- Your knowledge of the subject will inevitably increase as you develop the case and the logic flow from idea to outcomes.

- Your confidence will increase as you develop strategies to manage risk, recruit the best possible team, and assure that the design of your plan is sound.

- Your commitment to the vision grows as your confidence in the project, the plan, and the team increases.

- Your courage in presenting the case grows with your knowledge, confidence and belief in the project. As Margaret Truman said, "Courage is rarely reckless or foolish...courage usually involves a highly realistic estimate of the odds that must be faced".

By focusing diligently on the opportunity, you will automatically accrue knowledge, confidence, belief, commitment, and courage on the

"YOU" side of the scale. This is exactly what is required to balance the scale, and it can only occur by wholeheartedly developing the opportunity side. The point is that the "YOU" side is not about you at all. Rather it is what the audience receives from you as you communicate about the new plan. They will clearly see your passion and commitment to the vision and the outcomes it can generate.

If you find presenting to a group intimidating, the best cure is practice. Assemble a friendly group of close associates and ask them to give you honest feedback on your presentation. Deliver you presentation in front of a video camera and play it back to yourself. This will help you polish your delivery and also anticipate questions that might arise. Remember: You are not selling yourself or asking for help to save you from any difficulty. You are sharing an opportunity that has the potential to generate positive outcomes for the audience. Since you know your audience to be people who love a great opportunity, you are going into the situation with the expectation of success. This confidence will help you get the result you want. As Zig Ziglar talks about it, "Confidence is going after Moby Dick in a rowboat, and taking the tarter sauce with you—a bullfighter who goes in the ring with mustard on his sword."

Avoid "The Helicopter Plan"

Imagine building a staircase with one hundred steps. The foundation for each and every step must be sound in order to support the ascending steps. Clearly, once you build a solid foundation, your focus can easily shift to adding and climbing the remaining steps as fast as you can. Let's say after reaching the third step you seem to have got the hang of this process. You can now look forward and see exactly how the remainder of the steps will be built. For the first time, you have not only a clear vision of the end game but you can actually see how you are going to get there. Your confidence and enthusiasm have never been higher.

At this point, you have two choices to make. The wise choice would be to continue building the foundation and steps exactly as you now see them. Your experiences combined with the clarity you have gained along the path to the top have positioned you well for success. Or, you could let your enthusiasm turn into impatience and go for the shortcut—the helicopter plan. You let all of your prior judgment and planning fly out the window. Surprisingly, many leaders do this despite learning by experience that you can't skip steps. They see the end so clearly, they decide to jump from step three to step 42.

The helicopter flies high enough, so you can drop a tall pole that is the correct height for step 42. Then you climb out on top of it and celebrate the achievement. You are a hero! You have left all of those other suckers behind by soaring up while they slowly and doggedly build their stairs. Then you look up to step 43. Suddenly, you notice that in the gap between 42 and 43 there is a chasm. There is no foundation supporting 43 and guess what? There is no place for that helicopter to land to pick you up and try that pole trick again. Worse yet, you have discovered that the world had become a rather wobbly place. Balancing that tall, thin pole to keep it vertical to support you and your team and all the promises you have made to the marketplace is becoming a mighty challenge.

As Judi Adler said, "Champions know there are no shortcuts to the top. They climb the mountain one step at a time. They have no use for helicopters!" If a helicopter pilot and a mountain climber both reached the same summit, which one has the greater achievement? Which one has truly mastered the challenges of the mountain? The foundation of knowledge and experience under step 42 is an unstable and flimsy pole. It certainly cannot support adding more steps. Now you are stuck. You realize that in order to go forward, you have to go back and build the foundation that was required in steps four through 41. To add to the challenge, you have to keep step 42 afloat and balancing precariously while you go back and work on the earlier steps in the right order. Do you have sufficient resources to take all of this on, or will the effort cause you to falter permanently?

Assume you even make it back to step 42 with a new solid foundation beneath, you may find that you have to completely rebuild step 42 as well. This is because it was the wrong step, built on the wrong foundation. In order for it to play its proper role in helping you get to your goal—step 100—it will need to be rebuilt. Meanwhile you have customers, employees, investors, and a lot of other resources and expectations invested in the original promise of step 42. Getting all of that back on track with your new ("original") foundational steps is yet another challenge and resource drain.

What does The Helicopter Plan produce?

1. A major disruption and diversion away from a plan that had just become clear.

2. A major drain on resources as you go back and rebuild the foundation and earlier steps while keeping the new step going in some unplanned form.

3. A major drain on resources while you rebuild the step 42 and reset expectations leftover from your original plan.

When you try the helicopter plan, you always have to come back and work on the steps you missed. It takes twice the energy to do this and is very inefficient. Along the way, you will find that many of the steps you thought you had completed now have to be redone. Old "completed" steps may have been built on shaky ground and now need reworking. This rework causes you to spend time and energy that takes you away from making progress to the next step. The combination of rework and parallel working on steps at different stages can be a sufficient impedance to choke your project to a dead stop. Imagine if all those resources and time had been devoted to the original plan?

The old adage, "less haste, more speed" seems apt advice to people who consider that fateful helicopter plan choice. Large complex projects including: business startups, new ventures, product launches, and corporate branding initiatives can all benefit greatly from leadership that understands and commits to the idea that you need to slow down before you can accelerate. By diligently following the working plan you so carefully developed, you will be in a better position to go faster later on when it really counts. The kind of speed that powers the momentum to drive your business to success comes from a solid foundation that is built on planning, research, testing, practice, and commitment to stay with the program.

Sticking with the original plan also makes it easier to fine-tune your steps and make occasional course corrections. Certainly you need to adapt your plans, strategies and actions to changing conditions. You will have a far greater ability to adapt to change and stay in control of your plan if you stick with it. In the helicopter approach, what would happen if conditions changed while you were standing on your flimsy pole at step 42? You're barely staying upright and now you have to adapt to a change? By following through with all the steps in your plan you will:

1. Be prepared to accelerate and adapt to change when it really counts.

2. Make the most efficient use of resources to execute your project.

3. Avoid costly rework and parallel activities.

4. Significantly reduce the risk of failure and increase the assurance of success.

Every time you are tempted to take that helicopter shortcut, keep your feet on the ground. Make the choice to climb the mountain and get on with it!

CHAPTER SEVENTEEN

Measurement

Now that you've developed your plans for creating your brand and communicating it to the world, it's time to figure out which measurement techniques you will use to determine how well you are performing. Just as you planned your launch communication in three steps (employees, customers, and market), your measurement processes need to align with these three areas as well. The techniques for doing so will vary. For employees, you have the opportunity to maintain a continuous dialog with them and tie in reward and recognition systems. You can use interactive web-based surveys to get feedback on issues of any type. Added to that, you can conduct annual employee satisfaction surveys. All of these instruments should be aligned with your brand promise and vision, so you have a reliable way to take a real-time pulse of employee satisfaction, performance and alignment.

Customer measurements can similarly take the form of online, as well as telephone surveys to assess their satisfaction with your business and how well they believe you are living up to your brand promise. To get a real-time assessment, you should be asking how you are doing at every step along the way. That includes: after the purchase, as they interact with service support, after installing updates, and just about any contact they have with your business. Ask what they know about your company and what it stands for. You will gain tremendous insight into the effectiveness of your branding initiatives and promotional programs. For customer satisfaction surveys, you may find that contracting with and independent third-party will produce more objective results. Many companies form customer advisory boards—which include key customers and company executives. The advisory board meets about twice a year to discuss many business, product, service, and operational items. Such meetings can also serve to validate how well the company is performing across all areas in relation to the brand promise.

Awareness is defined as having knowledge of something because you have observed it or somebody has told you about it. When measuring market awareness and perceptions about your company's brand, there are several factors that need to be included. First you want to measure basic recognition. Have they heard of your company, and can they place it within the correct category of business? This awareness measurement is typically conducted in a two-tiered approach. The first tier is called unaided awareness, in which survey respondents are asked some questions about leading vendors of products within your category and they automatically recall names of companies that they associate with those products. Unaided awareness measures how many people manage to make the correct association about your company when you have not prompted them with any specific information. This awareness is the strongest and most valuable form of awareness. The second tier is called aided awareness which measures how many survey respondents failed to automatically think of your company unaided, but did recall your company name when prompted with bits of supporting information. When they recognize your company during this process—even with an "Of course, how could I forget?" comment—this is aided awareness.

In addition to assessing basic awareness of your company, your survey should assess various attributes of your brand to measure the respondents' perceptions about your business. This will include testing your Vision Statement or tag line, product and service quality, pricing, service and support responsiveness, adaptability, your strengths and weaknesses, and other relevant business operations. In addition, you will want to learn how they view your competition, is their customer experience better or worse or are they even aware of your competitors at all? These awareness surveys should be conducted, ideally, by independent service providers on an annual basis. Each year, as you re-examine your brand strategy, this analysis will be instrumental in providing guidance on the direction and actions you will choose to continue to lead your brand and your company successfully toward your vision.

ELEPHANT WALK
PATRICK SMYTH

Conclusion

The company vision is a statement about a new set of outcomes that your company is committed to creating for its customers. This vision is an enduring promise that is reflected in your brand promise and identity. This does not mean that your vision stays static over time, and it certainly does not mean that your brand is carved in stone either. The goal is not to align the company operations and employees with a brand strategy and then rigidly stick to that model forever. In these rapidly changing times and market conditions, a static approach could leave you completely out-of-step with the market and out-of-touch with your customers. Just as your products, services, and sales and marketing programs need to adapt to changing market needs and competitive pressures, your vision and brand need to adapt as well. Typically, the change-cycle for the vision and brand is on a longer loop than other elements.

The key point to remember is that the entire company, its people and processes, need to be realigned each time the vision and brand are adapted to meet a new opportunity. Most of the time, these will be small and fairly simple adjustments. Periodically, a major change is needed, and the effort to realign the company to the new positioning is substantially more complex. It's important that you recognize changes in the marketplace and the potential impact on your brand and vision, so you can better anticipate changes and keep your company aligned with its vision and purpose over time. Maintain a forward-looking process, refine your strategic plan and brand to effectively plan ahead.

Each day as the huge herd leaves their overnight resting place and each member, large and small, takes their last long drink for the day, they all fall in line behind the matriarch for the day's trek. They will cover as much as 40 miles in a day foraging for food. The matriarch always seems to know where she is going, and the herd trusts her to lead them safely to water before the end of the day. As they set off, the herd seamlessly splits into several pods of maybe a half-dozen elephants, each led by a younger female. These animals consume huge amounts of foliage daily, and splitting up allows them to spread the demand and make sure that each gets its fill. The pods will drift as far as 10 miles apart during the day. As we saw earlier, they are also capable of covering ground very quickly to come to the aid of a pod in distress.

Amazingly, there were no strategic planning sessions, no committee meetings, no memos circulated, no drawings of lots or organizational charts to figure out which animal went with which pod, who was going to lead it, where was it going to go, and how was it going to reconnect with the herd. Yet, at the end of the day, they all make it to the same resting place led by the same matriarch. In the Kalahari Desert, herds have been observed to cross 30 miles of sand dunes in a day to reach the next watering hole. Nothing but huge waves of red sand as far as the eye can see, and yet the elephants know where to go for water. Clearly, their ultra low frequency communication plays a huge role in helping them all stay connected. But there is so much more. Their instincts and learned behavior passed down over the years by experienced leaders prepares each generation of elephants to successfully demonstrate these awesome feats every day.

Their ability to navigate, adaptability and deftness in facing the challenges of each new day, and their power of affinity created by effective communication and trust in leadership demonstrate for us the power of alignment to a singular purpose. A lone elephant may not look like a finely-tuned well-oiled machine—like a cheetah might—but what they are capable of as a herd is nothing short of miraculous. They are a highly evolved, finely-tuned collection of animals that is a formidable and unchallenged force in the animal kingdom. This dedication to a purpose, alignment, affinity, communication, and exceptional performance is precisely what businesses can strive to achieve. It requires a clear and compelling vision, a brand strategy that is well aligned with that vision, a brand philosophy that achieves the maximum level of affinity with the customer community, and a relentless long-term commitment to making sure that every part of the business executes accordingly.

An elephant may not be the best dancer in the world, and you may not want to be near one if it started to try. But when it walks and does what it was designed to do, in concert with all of its teammates, the elephant exhibits exceptional powers of leadership, intelligence, endurance, and mastery over its domain. Keeping all of the different parts of your company aligned and focused on your brand promise can be very challenging. Errors and inconsistencies may already be causing your business to dance, thereby taking away precious resources from your ability to move forward efficiently. No doubt your competition is committed to throwing you off even more, making lift your feet higher and become increasingly unbalanced. If you keep your organization aligned you can fend off these efforts and be a formidable master of your domain. Does your business dance, or walk like the elephant—as a formidable force in your marketplace? As Abraham Lincoln said, "When you have got an elephant by the hind leg, and he is trying to run away, it's best to let him run." Be that elephant and your competition will not be able to keep up with your pace…or slow you down.

Index

C

D

E

F

About the Author

Patrick Smyth was born and raised in South Africa. As a young soldier in the South African army, he had the dubious privilege of meeting several members of the animal kingdom up close and face-to-face, but his encounters with elephants were his greatest source of inspiration and awe.

Patrick relocated to the US in 1981 and has led re-branding efforts and served as a senior marketing and business executive with several Fortune 500 companies including AT&T, Tandem Computers, Compaq Computers, Ceridian, and WebMD/ Emdeon.

Patrick continues to use his skills as a "leadership navigator," working with dozens of CEOs in small, high-growth businesses. His highly-acclaimed workshop helps people overcome their fears and self-limiting beliefs. Patrick is passionate about helping people be successful in their endeavors. In his own words, "I don't believe I have a right to step on someone's dream. Instead, I feel a duty to help them succeed."

He is a recognized speaker, author of many articles on leadership and an instructor and mentor at CEO Space Forum.

Patrick resides with his wife and teenaged son in a small town near Nashville, TN. He enjoys gardening, puzzles, golf and bass fishing when he has time.

ELEPHANT WALK
PATRICK SMYTH